M000235089

CTO
EXCELLENCE
IN 100 DAYS

CTO
EXCELLENCE
IN 100 DAYS

Becoming the Leader
Your Company Deserves

ETIENNE DE BRUIN

LIONCREST
PUBLISHING

COPYRIGHT © 2023 ETIENNE DE BRUIN

All rights reserved.

CTO EXCELLENCE IN 100 DAYS
Becoming the Leader Your Company Deserves

ISBN   978-1-5445-3832-7   *Hardcover*
       978-1-5445-3834-1   *Paperback*
       978-1-5445-3833-4   *Ebook*

CONTENTS

Introduction ix

PART ONE: BEFORE THE JOB, BUILD
A PERSONAL FOUNDATION..1

1. Find Yourself in the Role 3

2. Build Your Business Network 13

3. Nail the Interview..23

4. Build a Collaborative Partnership 39

PART TWO: 100 DAYS BY THE TENS........................53

5. Your Guide to Becoming a Successful CTO...........55

6. Days 1–10: Learn the Business Goals and Objectives...........59

7. Days 11–20: Learn to Socialize 67

8. Days 21–30: Set Goals 79

9. Days 31–40: Relate Personal Values
to Company Goals.. 91

10. Days 41–50: Understand Company Dynamics 105

11. Days 51–60: Use Flowcharts and Documentation 123

12. Days 61–70: Learn to Improvise 143

13. Days 71–80: Maintain Trusting Relationships 153

14. Days 81–90: Create "What If" Scenarios 163

15. Days 91–100: Understand What Is Truly
Important to Stakeholders 171

PART THREE: KNOWING THE ROPES
AND MOVING FORWARD 179

16. Work with Others..181

17. Consider the Role of Failure 195

18. Make a Great CTO... 205

Conclusion 213

Appendix 219

The Pelican Framework 219

Acknowledgments... 227

About the Author 229

Dedicated to Colette, Genevieve, and Jacques.

Wherever you go, Mommy and Daddy are right behind you.

We are a community of people seeking
excellence in our roles as CTOs

For more information on joining us
as well as continuously updated resources,
head over to https://ctoexcellence.com

INTRODUCTION

WHEN I TOLD MY TECHNOLOGY FRIENDS THAT I WAS WRITING a book about the first 100 days on the job as a Chief Technology Officer (CTO), I got the same response every time: "Why 100 days? It's always a 90-day plan." I've pushed the tried-and-tested plan up 10 days because there is an emotional connection to that number. It was also the first solid plan I witnessed when I came to America.

When my wife and I arrived in America in 2000, George W. Bush was running against Al Gore for president of the United States (POTUS). The race was in full swing, and it was two months from the November election. Televisions everywhere were lit up with debates, speeches, and ad campaigns. What struck me was how often they referred to their first 100 days in office. This first 100 days would set the tone for their full four years as president.

This inspired me to research the idea of the "first 100 days." My model of the first 100 days, which you see here, is based on the extraordinary accomplishments of another POTUS, Franklin D.

Roosevelt. He took office toward the end of what Milton Friedman called "the Great Contraction." It was a period kicked off by the infamous stock market crash of October 1929, which left the American people nervous and susceptible to rumors of the coming financial disaster. This period saw unemployment rise from 3 percent to 25 percent.

Franklin D. Roosevelt took office on March 4, 1933, and what he would do in the first 100 days of office would shape his legacy and his country. He needed to implement, innovate, and inspire while supporting the pillars of leadership, teamwork, timing, and technology. He took off from the runway, tempering his flight with the help of smartly appointed advisors. During his campaign speech, he stated, "Throughout the nation men and women, forgotten in the political philosophy of the Government, look to us here for guidance and for more equitable opportunity to share in the distribution of national wealth…I pledge myself to a new deal."

FDR's pledge set him on the path to a remarkable first 100 days. While you're not the president of a country, I find it inspirational to view your role as CTO as one of bringing remarkable change to the company you're joining. You are approaching the company with the tools it needs to help it succeed not only while you are there, but for years after you leave. You are using your first 100 days to deliver on your reputation, which has preceded you.

Being a great CTO isn't just about the first 100 days. It is about what you do before you get there, what you do while you're there, and what you leave behind. It is about the steps you take to become the best possible CTO and the actions you complete to support your words. The first 100 days for a CTO, similar to those of our most inspirational leaders, are for reshaping, reforming, and rebuilding wherever you are able. As a CTO, you have the power to create changes that will heal and strengthen a company from within.

This book will serve to show you how to throw out the "norms" and approach the job from a different angle. We will discuss the relationship between the CTO and the CEO. We will discuss a select few ways to get where you need to be, both personally and within the company, and how to navigate the C-suite to foster only the best ideas. We will review your first 100 days and help you leave a presidential impression on the companies with which you work.

MY LIFE BACKGROUND

I grew up in South Africa. I knew from the time I was a child in the eighties that I loved computers. In school, we used to have a computer lab with BBC computers. Two of my best friends and I would go to the computer lab to practice coding on every break or free period. There was an incredible atmosphere of coding and what coding can bring to all of us. The good feelings I got from coding with my friends fostered my passion for computers and technology.

I remember being ten years old and being drawn to the glowing screens of arcade games. In South Africa, there were cafés, which would be closer to liquor stores in America. The owners wanted to distinguish themselves from other cafés, so they would bring in the latest and greatest arcade games. The kids loved it. I had a lot of fun watching other kids play *Moon Patrol*,

Ms. Pacman, Galaga, and *Rally X,* as I was never good at playing them myself. I found myself more fascinated by how the games worked than just by the hedonistic fun my friends got from it. I wanted to know how everything moved on the screen. I was always asking, "How?" How does it work? How did they make it move that way? Why does it act this way?

I remember going to a friend's house where there was an Intellivision gaming console. I was entranced. His brother showed me a Walkman for the first time; Ultravox's "Vienna" was the first song I ever heard on a Walkman. The sound was everywhere, and I was amazed. Being in that home was a pivotal moment for me. I wanted to know how it all worked. I asked my parents for a gaming console, but they were wary of kids' fads. Instead of getting a console, I was sent to computer camp. I learned how to use an Atari 800, where I practiced computing with Logo. I was immediately hooked. My dad's "evil plan" to draw me away from gaming consoles to computers worked.

My family helped me buy my first computer, but first I had to prove that I was serious about using it. I saved all the quarters I would have spent at the arcade in envelopes. When they noticed my devotion to working toward a goal over frivolous spending, I got my computer. It was an Atari 800 XL. I started coding in Basic almost right away. I learned the basics, and the first day I figured out how to add two numbers in Basic and store them in a variable. I had my eureka moment and ran down the street in unbridled happiness.

From there, I started coding two programs. One was a program to keep track of my pocket money. My dad wanted me to use accounting practices to track money, but I wanted to optimize that idea. I tracked how much money I would get, how much I would spend, what I would spend it on, and how much I had left. The program drew graphs using the information. The second program helped track the Top 40 songs on the radio. Back then, you had to listen to the radio every Sunday to hear the Top 40 most popular songs for that week. I had to quickly track the songs, where they were on the charts, and how they were moving. I started to predict which songs were going to move up to number one using this program. Needless to say, my predictions were hit and miss, but here's the fun legacy that remains: I had more fun with my own Top 40 than with the one on the radio.

Unsurprisingly, I ended up majoring in computer science at university. It was here, in 1990, that I had my first encounter with the internet in the form of IRC. It was a chat app. Remember, in South Africa, we were part of the cultural boycott. We didn't get music, shows, CDs, anything, due to apartheid. I felt disconnected from the world. My favorite band was U2, and they had boycotted South Africa. My world was computers, and everything exciting in computers was happening overseas. All my heroes were overseas, so IRC helped me feel more like part of a global computer enthusiast club.

I graduated with a bachelor of science and with honors, then went to work with the Council for Scientific and Industrial Research (CSIR), where I built and ran our first IRC server, built an NNTP server, which served as South Africa's first Usenet server, and built out SSL relays and encryption device drivers. Eventually, a new company purchased our work, bought out my university scholarship—which had been granted by the CSIR— and brought me on board to work for them.

The new company, Nanoteq, was also located in South Africa and gave me an introduction to private startup enterprise.

I was pleased to be part of this air of possibility. At this time, South Africa was coming out of the apartheid regime. Most of my youth was characterized by the sanctions against South Africa. Computer magazines weren't sent to our stores; everything felt like an extra effort in my youth. My favorite computer was the Atari, and even those stopped being exported to South Africa. Software was difficult to find, so I was drawn to open source, modems, and anything I could find. After living with these restrictions, the freedom I found in the startup to build anything and do anything was intoxicating. Being a part of that startup had a profound impact on my life.

The entrepreneurial spirit awoke in me. I had a front row seat watching this company build itself on the world stage of network security and data encryption. I already had a taste of coding and knew what I loved in that area; now I had a taste of entrepreneurship and knew I wanted to make the two meet.

I found a role model while working at Nanoteq. His name was Jaco Botha. In him I saw a glimpse of my future, of who I wanted to be as a leader in an organization. Finding someone to emulate, who is successful and has a lot to teach, grounded my career and would eventually shape my future endeavors.

Jaco embodied incredible engineering intellect and strength. I recognized the strain the business took on him, yet he projected incredible grace when working with us. He was inspiring us to do our best. He wasn't our "buddy" at work, but he was a driving force that encouraged us to work our hardest without being too overbearing. I aspire to be that type of leader as a CTO and as an advisor to CTOs.

I married my wife around this time, and we began settling into life as newlyweds. Nanoteq was acquired by a private equity firm, which also acquired a German cryptographic organization called KryptoKom. We had an opportunity to move to a small border town in Germany called Aachen. As I was a key player in one of the projects being acquired, my wife and I decided to pack everything and move with a long-term view. We believed the world was our voice; South Africans were finally welcome to the world. It was an exciting time to be a South African postapartheid.

In 1998 we landed in Germany, and it was rough. Aachen felt like the final outpost for Germans at the Belgian and Dutch border, so the language and culture felt very closed to internationalization. You couldn't order a pastry without perfect German at the bakery. Movies were all dubbed into German. There weren't any English TV channels, and absolutely everything was in German. The first phrase I was taught in German was a protracted apology for not speaking German. We were young, naive, and scared, to a degree. While these were difficult times for us, I will cherish the three years we spent in Germany with all my heart.

The German company I joined was under tremendous pressure to release their newly acquired product. Regardless of this pressure, they were insistent on perfection. Our team really struggled. In fact, in the time I worked there, we hardly shipped any code I wrote because it wouldn't do exactly what the company wanted it to do. Others would have released it already, but this company wanted to get to the next big thing right on its first release. I began to see flaws in this type of thinking. I learned the wrong way to go about producing software and handling technology. While it was extremely frustrating, it was an important learning opportunity I did not take for granted.

With me miserable at work and my wife lonely and bored in a country where she couldn't legally work, we decided to relocate. I found a job with a biotech company in America, and we packed up and moved to San Diego.

When we moved from South Africa to Germany, a relocation service took care of our belongings. We did not have the same option during our move to America. We shipped a few boxes through the post office, and many of our things arrived broken. There was nothing mystical about our arrival in America.

However, my time at the biotech company incubated the entrepreneurial spirit that had begun all the way back in South Africa. My mentor from this company, who remains my dear friend today, showed me how to interact with others to generate the best possible outcome. The German company taught me what to avoid. Even if I didn't realize it at the time, I was building something in myself that would become incredibly useful for my future.

Although I loved my mentor, I grew to dislike the work and my boss. The whole work environment began to bother me, so I began turning my attention toward the internal employees. There were about 150, and I started building tools and little scripts that would make their lives easier.

For instance, they struggled with daily sales reports. They had this massive ERP system that was built on Oracle, and they would need someone in IT to run the weekly sales reports for them. They sent the report to the VP of sales so he could see what was going on. I figured out how to hack the Oracle database schema so I could extract data in real time instead of on a weekly basis. I used a PERL library to build a web page and put some graphs on there.

I drew immense satisfaction from this organization. I felt like I was doing a bit more, like I was doing something important for the company. The VP of sales accidentally stumbled onto my work and was floored by it. The real-time sales dashboard I was able to create was shocking because I could get all the right information hidden deep inside their own system.

The pivotal moment for me here was discovering that the simplest tools can have the greatest impact on people. This is where I realized I wanted to highlight software that makes people happy by saving them time and creating simpler processes. This is when the entrepreneurial interest that was bubbling beneath the surface finally came to light. At that time, the term CTO wasn't really a thing, but I knew that was the direction I wanted to go.

BECOMING A CTO

I soon became a technical co-founder when a friend of mine proposed building a content management service that helped nonprofits gain a web presence. We built a gorgeous first page for these organizations so they could get up and running quickly. It was a novel idea for the time, and it was successful.

My co-founder focused on the business and the growth while I focused on the technology. From here, I had to build a team. I had to hire people. Through our efforts, it became a multimillion-dollar company. I started getting asked to be an advisor to other founders. I started understanding my role as a CTO. It was still a role that was coagulating into something, but I was at its genesis. I was a bit of an anomaly. There simply weren't many of us in existence.

As I was still figuring out what my role as a CTO meant, I realized I encountered a difficult transition from coding to having a skill no one else had. In coding, everything is black and white. There is immediate feedback: it's either true or false. I built things that everyone wanted. In the role of the CTO, I had to work on non-coding skills that I wasn't sure other people would want.

It did something to my ego. As a technical co-founder, I literally opened a blank Vim session and started coding the product that would make this startup millions. With this expertise came a sense of entitlement, and I figured if I continued to do this, it would catapult me into the rest of my career. That is not what happened.

As you build your practice or your individual contributor skill, inevitably, you add people to it. These people need to be led. It's not difficult to lead a small group, or to lead if you're the smartest person in the room, but that model fails quickly as the group grows beyond that initial five or six people. Being the smartest in the room suddenly becomes a liability because the group can't grow beyond your weakness.

I didn't realize that I had begun accumulating skills that could be helpful to other people—not only to other CTOs, but to other founders and other CEOs. I started acquiring these skills on my own every day, and it was only in the later part of my time at the startup I helped create that I realized I could help other people.

I became a connector. I was a community builder as well as a technical expert. I was in love with the people, while my fellow CTOs weren't as dedicated to them. This made me different in my community. I became an organizer of the local Ruby meetup group, and I started the Golang group with a friend. I realized that finding people to hire meant being part of a community. It seemed to come easy for me. I found my passion in building communities wherever I went.

Finally, in 2011, I decided I wanted to connect with other CTOs to learn from them and help myself be a better CTO to my startup. This was the birth of 7CTOs, a peer group created for CTOs to help each other. As of this writing, I am still actively building 7CTOs, which has grown to 300-plus members worldwide. Our doors are open to any and all CTOs, VPEs, and technical co-founders who want to find their tribes. Head over to 7ctos.com and apply!

WHY I WANTED TO CREATE THIS BOOK

I wanted to create this book to talk directly to you, the CTO. I know most CTO-types come from a programming background and, in many cases, have been programmers since an early age. You have built products and services all your life, and you are most comfortable working with technology. Similarly to you, I have known what I want to do from an early age; I am also a technical person.

I have learned, through working with many CTOs, that there are key characteristics that drive phenomenal CTO leadership. I want to share these characteristics with you and help you learn how to develop them. I want to help you understand the role and responsibilities of a great CTO. I want to show you how to own the role of the CTO and how to remind the CEO of your role. Most importantly, I want you to understand the real role of the CTO.

This book is split into three parts. In the first part, I look at what you can do to set yourself up for great CTO opportunities. In the second, I walk you through a 100-day framework for how to excel in your CTO role. In the final part, I take a look at some challenges you may have to deal with day to day and offer you some tools to help you navigate those. Throughout the three parts of this book, I will help you show up with your power and with your sense. If you can do this, you can flip things a little bit, where you can say, "How can I help your company? It's not about me or who I am. It's not about my commitment. It's about my presence of mind, my management style." You need to be curious about how you can join with the company's uncertainty and navigate people through it.

I've seen positive outcomes from this mindset. At times, you will get high fives and amazing sessions; other times, you will have simply averted a disaster. Sometimes, the conversations will reveal more work to be done, and oftentimes, that work will fall on you. You want to weather the storm and survive it.

I want you to come away from this book with an understanding of how to have those difficult conversations. You have to be careful not to get resentful and passive-aggressive. Instead, you want to gently guide conversations to a solution. You want to provide overall value to the company, especially in the first 100 days. If you are relentless in positivity and providing continuous value, that will not only help you succeed with the company in front of you, but it will also give you the reputation you need to approach future companies.

I want you to come away from this book with a renewed confidence in yourself. I want you to know how to show businesses that you are there to do business and get results through a system of communication and innovation. Some companies may fawn over you and hold you to impossible standards; I want you to know how to help companies tone this down. While praise is great, you are not involved with the company to be put on a pedestal. You are present to help solve issues through team building and finding solutions. Therefore, you need to take back your power. Focus on the "why" of the company and be the person who takes the wheel.

I want you to come away from this book with a devotion to participating in the process that provides solutions to problems. This is the value that you bring, and I want you to know how to present that value to CEOs. Know what you can accomplish and what results you bring with you. That is the positivity. It is the compression of the coal that brings the diamond.

PART ONE

BEFORE THE JOB, BUILD A PERSONAL FOUNDATION

1

FIND YOURSELF IN THE ROLE

FINDING A CTO ROLE FITS INTO MANY SUBCATEGORIES OF this chapter because it involves different steps in time and different actions you take before you even start looking. Whether you are an engineer, entrepreneur, or musician, or a technical or nontechnical person, you'll need to obtain a solid amount of growth to move into the role of CTO. Even if you are an experienced CTO, you'll be the first to agree with me that the growth never stops. Just like technology innovation waits for no one!

Beyond just being the tech person, the CTO is a leader and an innovator. Some CTOs say simply, "I'm the tech person; just tell me what to do and I'll go get it done. Give me the budget and I'll make it happen." Some CTOs can't even ask for a budget or don't know how to work within the budgeting process. Other CTOs are super experienced, having scaled companies from inception to series A, B, C, or D, but now they find themselves inside a fledgling organization, and they aren't succeeding.

One common trait, though, is that as problem solvers, as innovators, as CTOs, we want to be successful. That success doesn't just depend on your expertise. It depends on the environment inside of which you're practicing your CTO greatness. Either way, we need to get out of the mindset of "the value that I bring is through what I know and understand about technology."

A close friend of mine heading up a significant department at Amazon once told me that when Amazon thinks about someone's success, it's not confined to the person's skills and experience, but also to the team or company that they're joining. Will the company they join help them be successful? Or, said differently, will the person succeed inside the new company culture?

Some CTOs face many challenges, including lack of executive presence, influence, and, in many cases, respect. If you combine these with the fact that many CTOs are introverted and of a supportive nature, it can be particularly hard for their ideas for improvement to be heard.

To galvanize the role of CTO, however, you need to become a first-class citizen of the C-suite. That is something that is critically important to establish before you walk into the role in any company. Are you ready to shoot yourself out of the cannon and be the highly visible CTO your company needs you to be?

I had a fascinating conversation with a mentor of mine named Dan Stoneman. We dug deep into the meaning of the *T* in CTO and how it could be a misnomer in this day and age. The premise was the phenomenon where your best engineers thrive in their individual contributor roles because they find joy and reward in finding needles in haystacks. Doing this well inevitably leads to their promotions, where they then need to manage people, keeping them inspired and on track.

Success is no longer about the needle but about the haystacks. How well do you prepare, optimize, and trim the haystacks so the needles are easier to find? Do you have the right elements in yourself to expand the *T* beyond the technical? As you look for a CTO role, learn to assess yourself and build on personable aspects of your personality. Consider how you handle small talk and learn how to do it while looking for a role.

SO IS THE ROLE OF CTO TECHNICAL, OR IS IT NONTECHNICAL?

This is an interesting question because the answer is yes and no. I have seen many CTOs take a nontraditional route into their careers; in a sense, the job found them. In the CTO sense, a nontechnical person might not have the background in programming or engineering but absolutely could understand the power of technology and how products can transform a business.

In fact, in many cases, I believe the nontechnical mind is less constrained by *how* something can be done when they have total freedom and confidence to know that something *can* be done. At the same time, the technical CTO arrives armed with a deep knowledge of existing technology, what it does for the company, and what it can do for the company.

One specific topic that comes up often when I talk to CTOs looking for new positions is how to learn new technologies as a means to make themselves more marketable. This is a red flag to me. This could mean you are either undervaluing your skills as a leader or creating a smoke screen when it comes to your skills. Eventually, it will be revealed that your actual skills do not match the ones you say you have.

While we exist in a discipline that requires continuous learning and growth, I would invest in learning and adaptation as a skill over whatever new hot technology adds sizzle to your résumé. In other words, if you are nontechnical and are drawn to the role of CTO, own it. If you are a technology geek that loves the CTO role, enjoy that. In the end, you will draw more people and more opportunities when you are your authentic self.

The idea is to merge both the technical and the nontechnical into a dynamic individual who can work with the technology as well as the people behind it. You perfect these skills as you search for a CTO role through your network. Not only do you keep up to date with technology when you talk to the right people in the field; you improve your soft skills as well.

Integrate yourself into whichever field you wish to work in to find where the most help is needed. Do you prefer to work with fresh new ideas that haven't seen the light of day yet? Get into startup business groups. Is your focus on taking products that already have a user base and expanding that into new revenues? Find ways to interact with the product managers and C-suites of businesses in that area. Finding a CTO position relies largely on your networking ability and the reputation you build for yourself as you build your social network.

Clearly, you need to be interested in people. You need to talk to people. You also need to understand the playbook and really try to understand how your target organization does business.

Who reports to whom? What's their history? How do they truly interact within their space?

A mistake we often make is that we don't look into the products of the company. For example, if you're interested in working for a particular hardware company, buy their hardware (unless it's a rocket ship). If there's a particular SaaS company you're interviewing for, sign up for their product. Most of them offer a trial period anyway. You'll build empathy for the product, and you'll gain a deeper understanding of the niche in which you'd be serving as CTO.

UNDERSTANDING YOUR EQ

You also need to nurture your emotional intelligence. Emotional intelligence is the ability to recognize and manage your own emotions while recognizing and influencing the emotions of others. This is not the intelligence quotient (IQ); it is the emotional quotient (EQ). Where IQ is static, EQ is fluid and is a strength in a good CTO.

When you begin by nurturing and strengthening your EQ, the whole process works out easier, from the interview, to self-evaluation, to trust building, to communication, to the nurturing and influencing process, to the process of making an impact. Working on your EQ while trying to land an interview will serve you throughout every step of helping a company succeed.

Placing extra focus on your own EQ during the job hunt is prudent because you're going through a period of change. Fluctuating circumstances lead to an increase in risk, which means emotions run at a higher level than usual. Keeping your own emotions in check could be the difference between landing your dream job or landing nothing. Let's take a closer look at EQ.

There are four quadrants in the emotional quotient model:

Self-awareness. This is your emotional awareness and your ability to know yourself. You understand your feelings and why they happen. As you practice this skill, you learn to recognize triggers that cause certain emotions. This includes an accurate self-assessment and an understanding of your strengths and weaknesses. Self-confidence and having faith in your abilities is here. Strength in this area helps you become more willing to put yourself out there.

Self-management. You control your emotions in this quadrant. There is plenty of room for growth here, and it is a lifelong exercise. You become goal-oriented and self-motivated, and keep working through setbacks. Transparency grows, and open conversations happen more often. You adapt to changes with ease, showing an outward resiliency with optimism. You prepare for success instead of imagining the worst.

Social awareness. Empathy is found in social awareness. You form connections with others and understand their emotions. You contribute openly to the group and demonstrate a strength in service. Active listening is apparent, and you have an organizational awareness with the ability to be aware of how you are being understood.

Relationship management. You demonstrate inspirational leadership when you work on this skill. You've become a mentor or a role model. You influence others and articulate ideas clearly. You have become versed in conflict management, and you are now a negotiator and leader. You recognize and support change, helping to make it happen. You develop your team and build on the strengths of others. Teamwork skills and collaboration improve.

Daniel Goleman, author of *Emotional Intelligence: Why It Can Matter More than IQ,* popularized the idea of emotional intelligence in 1995. He combined the above quadrants into two competences: personal and social.

Personal competence. This is created when self-awareness and self-management are strong. You recognize your own emotions and how they affect others; this allows you to recognize the emotions of others. You become competent in controlling and diffusing, when necessary, emotional situations.

Social competence. This is created when social awareness and relationship management are strong. You become a stronger leader and develop skills in others through social competence.

Say to yourself, *I am going to be aware of the fact that pulses are coming in the information that I am hearing and that things thrown at me will cause emotional responses.* Learn to self-evaluate without criticizing yourself. Own how you feel in each moment and assess it to make sure you have the right reaction to that feeling in the workplace. Understand that you will make mistakes that will serve as learning opportunities for next time. Be mindful of reactions and learn to observe those around you. Learn how to ask yourself questions such as, *For some reason, I feel agitated right now. What's going on? What triggered that?*

Learn to keep your ego in check as well. For example, learn to recognize your weaknesses and try to improve rather than expecting others around you to excuse you for your faults. For example, say to yourself, *Sometimes I can be super clumsy in trying to explain the complexity of solving a problem, and trust is being challenged. How do I regain it?* instead of *I gave them the information. I don't care whether they believe me or not, but it's the truth.* Redirect your thinking and try to approach the problem from a place of empathy, not a place of ego.

Use this self-awareness to assess yourself and learn how to react better next time. Developing a stronger EQ before the initial interview will give you stronger wins after you get the job. Use the social network you're building to help gain this strength.

Whenever I am in the interview phase, as I often am, I adopt the mindset that day 1 of my employment started with the very first interaction I had with the company. Whether you get to work with these people or not, you're building relationships that could have unexpected gems for your future self. Your sense of self and your being will leave an emotional response with everyone you meet. If you're able to remember that, then everything else will fall into place.

Identify your own emotions and evaluate what each emotion does to you. You are only human. Are you withdrawn when you meet new people? Are you unpleasant to be around because you lack confidence? Do you tend to overreact when you're angry? What happens when things don't go to plan? Do you fall apart? What are your triggers? Learn to recognize them and deal with them in the moment to increase your emotional intelligence and look more professional at work.

One exercise I suggest that increases emotional intelligence is to become the observer of what's happening right now. For instance, you might say, *I am the observer, who is watching an interaction between myself and the CEO. What am I seeing? What's happening? I see the CEO is doing all the talking. Is that good? Am I truly taking in the conversation, or am I distracted and fearful?* The exercise takes practice, but what you are doing is stepping outside of yourself to truly analyze your interactions.

On a much smaller scale, this exercise can be done through people watching. Go to a park or busy shopping center and sit on a bench. Discreetly watch the people around you. How are they interacting with each other? What do you think is happening? What emotions are they feeling? Make up a little story about them in your head.

The more you practice this, the better able you are to turn it around on yourself and gain an outsider's view on your own interactions. Over time, you'll begin to notice yourself applying the same ideas to your own interactions. How are we interacting with each other? What is happening here? What emotions are we each feeling?

In this chapter we took a look at how important it is to be comfortable in your role as CTO. Whatever your passion, you will be a great CTO when you understand where your strengths help the company and where it is better to hire for complementing skills. You also saw the good news of investing in your emotional intelligence. This is an industry standard for being the world-class leader every company deserves.

Now, for this next chapter, let's take a look at how valuable you'll be inside your company by investing in activities outside your company.

2

BUILD YOUR
BUSINESS NETWORK

ONE OF THE QUESTIONS I LIKE TO ASK A CTO IS "HOW WELL developed is your network?" Describe your network. How many people would respond to an email or text from you? Here's an even better question: "How often are you the recipient of an introduction?" Maintaining a strong business network is often the part of being a CTO that is most malnourished. The best way to complete this maintenance is by offering help to others, which is covered in the "Essential Consulting" section.

Build your network by making smart choices, both in person and online. A good rule of thumb is to post only things you would say directly to someone's face in a professional setting. Think of every Slack message as being read while someone is parking their car. What about emails that clog up your recipient's inbox?

We've all been there before, writing that long email explaining a certain situation to someone. I think of every word in an email as an opportunity to be misunderstood by the reader. Think about how you read long emails. What do you see? How are your eyeballs drawn to certain words that stand out and shape your bias about the tone of the email?

I helped a CTO once who made a notable mistake on LinkedIn. He had spent the better part of twelve months out of a job and was becoming more careless in his posts. He finally made it to the final round of interviews for a job he really wanted. But after it became clear to him that the CEO wasn't up to speed on the role of a CTO, he became verbal and frustrated. He was failing to mind his EQ, especially self-management. He began posting his reaction to the interview process on LinkedIn.

Although he took great care to anonymize his posts, he ignored self-management and let the self-awareness of his negative emotions flow through his posts. The result wasn't great. He didn't use bad language, but he took an apparent stance with his opinion of how CEOs handled the process of partnering with a CTO. What happens to these posts when he eventually lands a position as CTO? Or, of greater concern, what happens to these posts when the HR department of a company scrolls through his LinkedIn profile and sees these posts?

In the end, the company passed on him. We'll never know if it was because they were aware of his LinkedIn posts, but my guess is they were scanning his profile and saw them.

When you are talking to a company about becoming their CTO, they will most definitely look at your online activity. They want to know if you are authentic in your conversations with them.

Imagine talking to a CEO about a partnership to help build his or her company. Imagine that conversation going really well. Later, the same CEO looks at your LinkedIn profile and reads messages you wrote criticizing how CEOs constantly put pressure on CTOs to perform.

You've put the idea of hiring a CTO into the CEO's head, but he or she will now question whether they will run into the same issues when working with you that you stated in your social media posts. Always remain professional and positive on social media. Save the frustrations for your personal diary or your closest friend.

Remember that 51 percent of the process is helping the CEO understand that they can trust you. Trust only comes when we feel we are interacting with someone authentic. If you're nice to the CEO's face but slam the position anywhere else, it's going to hurt you. Remember that networking is where you play the role of facilitator and demonstrate your leadership skills. Ask yourself, *Do I have the skills necessary to influence people and make them trust me?* It's less about your skill as a coder and what you've built in the past and more about trust and leadership.

Constantly look at nurturing your network. Another way I like to nurture my network is through a little game I created called "Reply Roulette." I will do a random search through my archived emails and look through older results, looking for people with whom I might have lost touch. Sometimes I find people with whom I did not follow up due to their message falling through the cracks, or through an email bankruptcy declaration. I use this opportunity and exercise to send out an introductory email just to say hello and to ask for an update from them. It's a great way to stay in touch, and I have had some opportunities reignite from this practice.

Here's a sample reconnection email:

> Subject: Resolved
>
> Hello Claire,
>
> I hope all is well with you and your company, ACME Pools. I came across one of your ads the other day, and it reminded me of the great conversation we had back in April.
>
> I recall some technical issues you were running into, and I'd love to know how you eventually got them resolved. Please let me know if you'd like to catch up. I have time next Friday.
>
> Sincerely,
> Ray

You've offered to reconnect with a suggested time frame. Since it's an email, you've given Claire the chance to opt out by not responding. You also may need to provide more of a "memory jogger" if it's been a long time since you last connected, so use this sample as a basic framework for the actual email. Enjoy Reply Roulette and let me know how it goes!

It's important to keep your natural network flowing. Make sure you have many options and many conversations. Offer help to people and practice generosity with your time. Remember that your help doesn't necessarily need to translate into dollar signs because it serves the greater good of nurturing your network and career.

Use caution in offering help to those who would exploit you, as explained in "Essential Consulting" (later on in this book), but do offer help to genuine businesses to help expand your career. Become someone that the C-suite of a company would be proud to have on their team.

Elon Musk was once asked what he admired about Steve Jobs. He responded that Jobs would probably be known for his products, but ultimately, Musk admired him for the team he was able to pull together. "The ability to attract and motivate great people is critical to the success of a company, because a company is just a group of people that are assembled to create a product or service."

In my mind, I am always asking myself, *How do I position myself so people want me on their team?* Get to a place where people want you on their team and you can start naming your price.

I make sure my actions, help, and technical expertise are always in service to the team so the team will consider asking me to join them when the time is right. To me, it is way more fun to orchestrate that than to put myself at someone else's mercy. I will position it as, "Hey, I had this crazy idea that will help you solve the problem you're having. If you're interested in working with me, we can make that happen." Do this over and over, keeping your network strong and helping others build confidence in your skills.

CONFERENCES AND NETWORKING EVENTS

There are many conferences and networking events that are great opportunities to meet new people and expand your network. You should go to as many as you can, but only with eyes wide open, as the shotgun approach can be quite fatiguing. Local networking events often attract the same groups of people, which does not help you much with expanding your network. When you attend these events, do not show up to sell yourself. Show up to offer your help and expertise.

Conferences can be incredibly difficult to navigate, even for the raging extrovert. I once went to a CTO Connection event in New York City, and I can't tell you how out of place and awkward I felt. I had no reason to feel this way, but I just could not work my way into any conversation, and it was driving me nuts. I have a few tips for you if you find yourself lost in your awkwardness.

Look for the other lonely person. By now you've probably seen somebody else who seems out of place and is not connecting with others. Hey, you have nothing to lose, so head over to them and share a few things about yourself. I find it's better to introduce and share a few nuggets about yourself before peppering the victim with questions.

It takes courage to talk about yourself, but do it. I used to teach my daughter to find the loneliest kid on the playground and to go make friends. You never know who you might be meeting and the impact you'll have on their lives.

Another idea is to secretly pick up the tab at the bar. I am regularly amazed at how manageable the tab is for a small group of people hanging out at a meetup. Event organizers are usually blown away that someone shows such empathy for their stress levels. And here's the kicker: you'll pick up an advocate or two.

Whether it be the barperson pointing at you in response to the organizer asking who the mysterious donor was or a few of the patrons who happen to see you do the deed, you'll feel amazing, and the mystery will serve you well. Please note, I am not suggesting that you pick up the tab and then triumphantly jump onto the bar counter to announce your arrival.

It's always easier to connect with a stranger when the object of the conversation is outside of the exchange. Even asking your target where the restrooms are opens a door for some connection later in the day. "Hey, do you mind telling me where the next session will be held?" or "Did you happen to catch the speaker's reference to his dog's name?" or "Do you know where the happy hour will be later tonight?" are all legit questions seeking legit answers, but also building a hair of a connection between you and your potential new best friend.

ESSENTIAL CONSULTING

Through your networking, you have met people who may need your services. Offer them consulting services to get to know them better. It's a "try before you buy" program for the C-suite. Work on projects together to see how things go. I am a huge fan of this method because it's like dating. The trap we fall into, though, is not imagining what success or failure looks like, so we wind up just plugging along. Work on keeping things simple, uncomplicated, and fluid.

I found an opportunity to consult through my network when I was approached to help a company navigate some challenges around the pending exit of their lead engineer. They basically wanted to know what the role was of a VP of engineering or a CTO so that they could formulate their new hire strategy.

It's always fun to give advice because you have nothing to lose if you are genuine and sincere in the help you provide. I usually go straight for the relationships when meeting delegations like this so that I can build a level of trust before imparting any wisdom I might have.

Another reason to offer your casual help is that there are no forced constraints around expectations, availability, and remuneration, which allows for an honest and authentic relationship to be forged. And then, of course, if the thrill goes away or you gradually stop meeting, no harm, no foul. I do like to follow up every once in a while, though.

Following up after offering consultation services helps you understand how they are doing, it helps you improve your skills, and mostly, it helps your timing in getting a CTO position.

Keeping in touch with the companies with whom you consult gives you an inside look into when they're ready to hire. They already know you and hopefully already like you, so you have a bigger shot at landing the job. When they seem ready to hire, throw your hat into the ring. I've used this method in the past, and it has led me directly to the interviewing process.

The "giving mindset" is the key to landing paying CTO work. It's not who you help, and it's not who you network with that is the end. That is a means to an end. You really are networking with the people they know and the problems they're trying to solve. I have a friend in Silicon Valley who is a giant in my life in terms of the leads he sends me. He called me on a Wednesday to say that he was considering acquiring a company and he really needed to know if the tech that he was purchasing was worth the investment. He asked for my help in understanding the technology and in making sure it was sustainable for the future. I jumped at the chance to consult with him.

The next thing he said was, "The catch is that we have a call scheduled for tomorrow morning, 5:00 a.m. your time." My next internal question was, *Man, am I going to be able to do a good job for him? How do I brand myself through this so I look like I know what I'm talking about?* But I realized in that moment that I had to say yes first. Sometimes, it works to say yes first, and the rest will follow.

I ended up having an hour-and-a-half-long conversation with his team and the target company. I was able to deliver value without asking for a fee or negotiating a price. Even at my level of expertise, I still recognize the importance of maintaining my network through essential consulting.

This doesn't mean that you always say yes right away. Essential consulting is done carefully and is calculated not only by its value to you but by the person who is asking for help. Not everyone is in your corner, and not everyone will give you the same level of devotion you give them. You may have to make people negotiate to earn your time. Get to the yes quickly for those in your network on whom you can rely, then measure the rest to determine how fast yes happens.

There are some people who will try and exploit you, and for those people, I take longer to accept. For instance, I might wait for the second email they send. Another thing that's very difficult in establishing your network is the careless introduction. There are some people who spend that capital all day long. They are like, "Oh, Etienne is a CTO, and you are a founder. And I want to introduce the two of you to each other, because Etienne can help you." I really can't stand those emails, because it puts me on the hook in an involuntary way. I am the expert, I have been introduced, and this guy introduced me to make him look good because he knows someone: "Oh, I know the founder of so and so."

This is a good time to remind you to not do the same to people in your network. Always ask your experts before making introductions such as these. For example, if your company needs a designer, mention that you know someone without using names. Ask your network of designers if any are available, and then set up meetings with those who say they are. It may involve extra steps, but it is worth it to avoid creating situations where people are slow to respond to you.

In this chapter we took a look at the impact your reputation can have on your current job as well as job openings you're entertaining. We looked at taking tremendous care in how you are perceived by others and the idea that being helpful is the key to expanding your network. While we focus on helping others, we are bound to pique the interest of companies who will approach us and present us with new opportunities. Next up, we'll take a look at how to engage those companies.

3

NAIL THE INTERVIEW

CONGRATULATIONS! YOU HAVE A COMPANY INTERESTED IN your services. They've heard about you through your network, and they're excited to talk to you. They've requested an interview. The first thing to remember about the interview process is that your aim is to convince the CEO that you already have possible solutions for the company's issues.

Think of it this way. Let's say a company wants to grow from $2 million to $10 million as a startup. You want to be able to say, "Well, I'm the CTO who will help you get from $2 million to $10 million," as opposed to saying, "Well, I'm here to make sure the technology is in place for that growth." These sentences are the difference between the small CTO and the Scaling CTO. Make your intentions clear with the CEO right away. Let the CEO know how you see yourself working with them in collaboration for this growth.

The interview stage of the CTO position must be approached with a success mindset. Be confident in your ability to help the C-suite understand they can trust you in your role. Always work under the assumption that someone is happy to be working with you and that they are impressed with you. If they weren't impressed, you wouldn't be meeting with them to discuss work options. Operate under the assumption that those around you value you for what you know and for what you can do for their company as long as you give them 100 percent.

Remember that you are not coming in from the bottom and saying, "Please, I want to be your CTO because I want to help you with a few things." No, you need to come in with, "There's no other person you'd rather work with than me because I've demonstrated value, I've given you my time, I've floated some free ideas your way, and you've learned you can trust me."

Through your networking and essential consulting, you have proven that you are collaborative, open, and available. Leave no doubt as to how it would be to work with you. Help the CEO believe that his or her daily life will be better with you in it. Remember to stay in the success mindset and in the partner mindset, never in the "the CEO is my boss" mindset.

Approach the interview not thinking, *Let's see if we like each other, and then you will pay me*, but instead adopt the attitude of *I'm intrigued by your challenge. Let's have a conversation.* It must be an equal conversation in which you are making mental notes of the situation. You're learning where the company issues lie, and you're mentally assessing where you can help. This is not the time when you are trying to fix things, and it's not an hour used to impress someone; this is an hour used to gather information to fix things in the future. This will become your follow-up strategy. For example, you can say during a follow-up,

"Hey Sally, you mentioned the other day that you've got an issue with quality delivery. I know some people who might consult with you to help you improve in that area, if you're interested." You're finding problems and then providing solutions to prove your worth.

Wait to talk about things such as salary and equity in the company until it's either asked for or until you've been offered the position. The interview stage is for building on the trust you started in the consulting stage, building on the reputation that preceded you, and helping the CEO believe that the connection you're creating will benefit him or her. Having said that, I do like to name my own price when offering my consulting services.

With all that in mind, let's discuss the interview process. We will use a company with which I've interviewed as a sample. I chose to leave no stone unturned to illustrate how cumbersome the interview process can be. See if you can find yourself in this process and consider how you would have responded differently. I certainly hope you would have handled things differently!

The company I interviewed with was a $15 million per year revenue company looking to expand quickly to $50 million per year. They had an aging Ruby on Rails monolithic app, which meant that updates and improvements became harder and harder to make. They had a team of about fifteen software developers spread into three functional areas: one for implementation of their software, one for custom integrations post-sales, and one dedicated to their web-specific projects.

THE CASUAL CONVERSATION

My interview started with a casual conversation with the founder, who seemed to like me off the bat. She was a ball-buster, and I think she mostly wanted to see how we'd do with idea bantering or process improvement conversations. She was also mostly concerned with how I would roll out of some time commitments I had made in my run-up into the job market. All in all, it was a great conversation, which led me to the next step.

MORE CONVERSATIONS

The next step was to talk to her co-founder, who was operating in a COO role but was instrumental in leading the company's business development and sales efforts. He was very busy and distracted, and our conversation was limited to a quick intro-duction in the corridor. I often wonder if his lack of attention to me was a reflection of how he saw the role: just someone to get the IT stuff done.

PHONE SCREENING

The next step was a phone screen in which I spoke with the HR director and, while we didn't have any real personal rapport with each other, it went well. She was mostly interested in me sending her my salary requirements, to which I answered, "I'm looking at compensation befitting the C-suite of your company." I think that went down well. She also sheepishly asked me for my résumé at this point, and I used an app that converted my LinkedIn profile to a résumé.

I remember the CEO questioning me on this practice, saying that the résumé felt template-ish. At the time I thought it was sufficient because we had moved way beyond a blind interview, but in retrospect, I agree with her and think we should put more effort into our résumés. Hire a résumé writer and make your résumé something you would be proud to hand to anyone at any moment.

THE WATTERSON ASSESSMENT

Next, I received an email from the HR director asking me to complete a Watterson assessment. It was a cumbersome and time-intensive process to complete, but the results were worth the effort. Phrases like "This candidate demonstrates a very high capacity to solve problems, learn rapidly, and manage abstract concepts well" and "His critical thinking skills are quite strong, and in most circumstances, he is very open to alternatives and possibilities. In fact, he has a keen eye for observing details or aspects of a situation that appear to be out of place or which may not fit with the rest of the plan."

This made me feel very good about myself, and I was starting to think I was a highly valued candidate for this role. The Watterson assessment was particularly interesting because it also stated some possible interview questions, like "How does he keep himself intellectually challenged?" and "Will the activities of this role keep him challenged or is he going to become easily bored, perhaps frustrated?"

At this point, it is probably helpful to state that the person I was looking to replace had accepted a position with a larger company, and he still had a hand in all the code. While I greatly respect that, I had not anticipated coding prowess being part of the role of CTO for this company. I, too, am a coder, but I was not going to help this company grow by submitting my own pull requests. Last time I did that, my engineers politely filibustered me by commenting ad nauseum on my request with "clarifying questions."

THE HACKERRANK ENGINEERING TEST

My next mission was to complete a HackerRank "engineering test." The test was set up by the outgoing VP of engineering, and I couldn't tell if he was trying to stick it to me, but asking me to write nested SQL and async JavaScript functions didn't feel particularly relevant. The test took over two hours, and I didn't think I did well on it. You know how it feels when you dream that you're standing naked in your CS 101 class? That's how I felt.

After I took the test, I wrote the HR director the following email:

> I just finished the coding test. STRESSER! I'll confess that I'm a bit rusty but had fun, nevertheless.

I remember writing that email and thinking that I should just not take myself too seriously and hopefully gently enlighten them to the fact that some stress was involved when I did the test. I got the following response one day later:

> Thank you for completing this assessment so quickly; we appreciate it!

This response made me think about how important response times can be. It helped shape my ideas around setting the pace as a leader.

MEETING MORE DIRECTORS

The next step was an interview with two of the engineering directors. I breezed through that interview, and I felt like I had made two new friends, when I really hadn't. The mantra in my head was to not rely too much on my raging extrovert skills but to play it calmly, and I thought it had worked.

Later in the day, after a tour of the office and casual introductions to everyone, it was time to meet with the larger executive team. The hour had come. I was counted worthy and ready to meet my greatest challenge. They would all have my Watterson assessment and my résumé and be armed with questions pertaining to each of their functional areas. It was a large team, which included the CEO, the HR director, the newly hired COO, the VP of sales, the VP of marketing, the co-founder business development person, and perhaps one or two more.

This was a two-hour meeting that saw the sun set on us and the office lights grow bright. It was an important meeting because despite all the answers I gave that caused mutual laughter and approval in the CEO's eyes, saying, "You're doing great!" this was also the meeting in which I said something that killed the whole prospect for me and led to my disqualification from the process. Of course, it wasn't immediately obvious, and that wasn't shared with me until I went through two more steps.

FURTHER MEETUPS

I received an email shortly after my meeting with the executives saying that they loved meeting with me and that they would like for me to meet with a newly hired executive, since he wasn't in the group meeting, and we were probably going to work closely together. I saw this as a sign that I had executive approval to start getting into more detail. We met, we had a great time, and I thought this was a done deal.

MEETING THE TEAM

I received a thank-you email from the HR director asking me if I could break down a one-year plan for the company as a CTO. I felt good about this request since it felt congruent with the meetings we just had, and again it felt like we were getting into work mode. I promptly drew her a few pie charts and timelines in an expedited manner.

What followed was a curious two to three weeks of silence. I sent an email asking for an update when I couldn't wait anymore. After another uncomfortable wait time, I got an email back:

> Would you be available on either Monday or Tuesday to meet some of the other web developers for lunch?

I didn't understand. How was this relevant to the process? My ego was bruised. I thought, *Who do they think they're dealing with here?* I replied, too soon, with an email asking for clarification:

> What would be the purpose of meeting more people? Perhaps I need some clarification on where we are in the process.

One week later I received the following email from the HR director:

> Unfortunately, we have decided not to move forward with the next step of the process with you. This is due to the pushback that was given when I contacted you to schedule the lunch with the development team. We view this as an integral part of our interview process as this is a team that the CTO is going to be working closely with. This step was discussed when you last interviewed with us and so your response was fairly surprising and a determining factor in us not wanting to move forward. We do appreciate the time that you've taken to meet with us and wish you much success for the future.

Just like that, the process was over. I felt bruised and unhappy, but I was almost okay with my misstep. What I wasn't okay with was not knowing the real reason for my rejection. This didn't feel like the real reason, and as it turns out, it wasn't.

WHAT NOT TO SAY

A few weeks later, I saw via LinkedIn that a new CTO had been appointed to the company, and I felt relieved that perhaps it was just a better candidate who'd come along, and that is where I left it for a few months. I eventually reached out to the CEO to congratulate her on their new CTO and casually asked how things were going. She said that he was working out great and that she wanted to grab coffee with me. I accepted, and we met.

After some time, I saw an opportunity to ask about my sudden dismissal from the interview. Her response blew my mind. It happened during the executive leadership interview. She told me that some members of the team were concerned about a personal issue I had brought up. This issue wasn't even current, but it was a troubling overshare.

During the course of the interview, we began talking about our personal lives. The room felt laid back and warm, so I dove into my family life. I discussed our troubles conceiving and then talked about my vasectomy after having three kids. That overshare is what killed me. The C-suite worried how I would come across to the rest of the team if I was such an oversharer.

I didn't know whether to laugh or cry with relief. I was thankful to know that I was fired from the interview because of a personal story rather than professional competence. This experience showed me the value of playing your cards closer to your chest during the interview process. I relied on my dashing personality too much and let my guard down too far. I had forgotten the sage advice of my father: "Answer the questions they ask you and not the ones they never ask." In retrospect, I would have built the same rapport by lightly delving into my personal life and not verbally vormiting.

Remember to read the room. Learn everything you can about body language. A person who is engaged will lean forward and look at you. They will smile, and their hands will be apart from each other, as if they are welcoming the message into their personal space. When a person starts to get uncomfortable, they will lean away, rub their face, start to frown, look elsewhere, shuffle papers, or cross their arms. They are closing themselves off from the conversation and literally trying to protect their personal space from the information. Learn to recognize the signs of a person who is put off by your conversation to save yourself from the same embarrassment I endured. There are plenty of YouTube videos showing how this looks in real time. Learn to use body language and small talk to your advantage.

A few months later, I was talking to a friend of mine who had just taken a CTO role at a publicly traded company. He wasn't aware of the long process I went through and started explaining the same experience I had. I was pleasantly surprised that he went through the process, and I felt a sense of validation for my experience. I learned an important lesson about the executive hiring process, and now I embrace every step with patience.

NEGOTIATIONS

After you've impressed the C-suite and proven your worth as a partner, it's time to discuss negotiating your salary and expectations. As you will remember, when I was asked for my salary requirements during the interviewing process above, I did not give a direct answer. This is because I was still in the process of convincing them that they needed me. Your salary is not a simple answer, but something that must be negotiated until everyone is happy. It is also based on the fact that you are a partner, not an employee.

I was having a discussion with a close friend of mine one day when we were both in the house-buying process. He dropped a knowledge bomb about negotiating the deal that, to this day, I think about when considering salary negotiations. Since finding a house can be so cumbersome, it is tempting to overlook the "deal" when you eventually do find your dream house. He said that you had to be willing to walk away from a bad deal, no matter how gorgeous that house seemed. You can have a great house but a bad deal. Walk away from that house. The same goes for jobs: you can have a great job but a bad deal. That is why I always negotiate a great deal and walk away from the bad deals.

This is where understanding the company's financial goals comes into play. You need to know what types of products are creating what type of revenue, the company's overall goals, and how you will work next to the CEO to push the company into the future. All this contributes to the type of package you can negotiate for yourself.

As CTOs, we need to project our impact on the business value and then price ourselves accordingly. As a rule of thumb, I like to see a budget for technology that is in the 20–30 percent range of revenues. Something to consider in regard to the budget allocated for technology is the fact that the budget number indicates how much they value technology in the company.

Sometimes, if they devalue the technology contribution, they will have a smaller percentage allocated to it. That means that when I come to negotiate my salary, I need to keep that ratio in mind. If I'm asking for, let's say, $300,000, they may say, "Well, that's the total of our whole IT budget." Therefore, it is essential to know the company's annual revenues. Understand their product ranges and which ones are contributing most to the revenue. Understanding these numbers will not only help you negotiate your salary, but it will also help you know if you even want to continue with the company.

Remember, too, that you are a member of the C-suite. Consider the salaries of the other C-suite members. Do not fall into the trap of limiting yourself and reducing your value through your knowledge of the budgets or C-suite salaries. You should squarely position yourself and say, "Given the budget, given the revenue earnings, and given its product range, I believe that we can take this company to two times the revenue within twenty-four months." Price yourself accordingly.

Arrive at the negotiations with this information and push forward. Tell the CEO, "This is how I think technology can help us with pricing plans and churn rates and do all kinds of things. If we double revenues, I've just created a whole bunch of space for you in your operating budget." So the salary needs to be an upfront bet that you are going to get that done. Maybe you shave a little bit off your number, just to show them how serious you are.

I like to push the envelope. I operate under the assumption that I undervalue my skills, so I try to set the package myself. I don't try to say, "What would I pay myself?" because then I would undervalue that.

I think it's essential to look at a company's current financial strength and how you will enhance it. Then reverse that back into, "Well, in that scenario, when I accomplish my goals, the amount they're paying me is actually really small." Value yourself and price yourself to a two- or three-year goal that you'd like to accomplish at the organization. Then focus on potentially seeing if you can participate in the upside. For instance, say, "I'm willing to take this type of salary, but if we hit milestones A, B, and C, I would like to see a corresponding bonus or corresponding increase in my salary."

CTOs are often asked to do more with less. We're often asked to work harder and faster, delivering at the highest velocity. We must think about the resources in our coding jobs, be mindful of computing power, disk space, processing power, and everything it takes to build software. We become very good at working with scarcity and imagining how to do more with fewer resources. When we look at our role as CTO in the organization, we need to adopt that same mentality of "I am a resource of which there is a scarcity."

Remember that a bonus structure is fairly standard for CEO and CFO roles. It should become standard for the CTO role as well. For example, if the company is a $5 million company but doesn't pay any of their C-suite $300,000, that doesn't matter to me. I know that they're a $5 million company and I'm asking them for a small percentage of their annual revenues to pay for me.

Value yourself, and in order to value yourself you need to understand the business, its growth, and its revenues. I generally am not too hung up on equity. Equity is a tough one because it only rarely gets realized when there's an equity event or a liquidity event. Don't throw equity out, however. Equity in a company is common as part of a salary package, especially with startups.

Just be mindful when negotiating on terms of equity. If you want to negotiate 2 percent ownership in the company, for example, and they sell for $50 million, you're only going to get $1 million. So you need to ask yourself, *What if I work there for four or five years and my payout is $1 million. Is that why I'm doing this?* Sometimes the upside and possible downside of equity is when the company sells—not necessarily the salary you earned there.

Don't get hung up on equity, however. Get hung up on valuing yourself. I have a risky little rule of thumb for this. I want to be in a situation where someone wants to give me equity, because equity is not mine to ask for; it's theirs to give. If you engage in an elaborate conversation about the transfer of equity, you're fighting over something that's not yours to ask for. You haven't proven yourself; you don't know if the relationship's going to work, and things can change. You're asking someone to bet on the future even if they are four-year vesting and one-year cliff. It's far better to put yourself in a position where the company wants to give you the equity.

I find that people get hung up on the idea of equity too often. A better approach is to go for a high salary and consider equity a gift that comes later. Put your money where your mouth is by getting to a place where the company can't live without you and wants to offer you more. Eventually, you will be able to be pickier about where you work, whom you work with, and what you accept in compensation packages.

When you know that you're pricing yourself at your best personal value, and you position yourself at that value, but they don't see it, that's okay too. It might mean that this company wasn't the best option for you and it's time to walk away.

WHEN TO WALK AWAY

There is a time to walk away from a negotiation. When the CEO refuses to see you as an equal, and you cannot change his or her way of thinking, walk away. When the company refuses your salary negotiations after a few back-and-forths, and you know they have the financial ability to meet you in the middle, walk away.

You gain incredible power in the negotiation seat if you are willing to walk away. What you're communicating to the CEO is, "Listen, I am suggesting something for you that I believe is the right thing for your company. I believe in that so strongly that I do not *need* to be a part of it. I *want* to be a part of it. But my recommendation and counsel puts the company first and puts me and my interest second."

If the company can see that for what it's worth, and if you can be genuinely authentic about it, they might take your advice and run, or they might say, "Okay, well, thank you for your advice. We're done with you." If you can live with the discomfort of possibly having to walk away, you hold the reins and are stronger in negotiations.

Another reason to walk away is when you're being asked to pull off a miracle. I was once asked to step in and help get a release out the door that had been stuck for over a year. I relished the opportunity to step in and get the job done. I failed.

In this chapter we saw that the dance with a new company is a delicate one. It leaves no room for assumptions and certainly does not respect overconfidence. We saw that the interview process can be a long and drawn-out one and that you shouldn't attach any meaning to that. It is simply a long process. I am a firm believer in timing. And in due time, you'll find the right match.

Next up, we'll take a look at how to prepare yourself in the weeks running up to joining your new company.

4

BUILD A COLLABORATIVE PARTNERSHIP

You've demonstrated that you're not trying to have the whole pie to yourself, their needs are above your own, and you are gregarious in connections and helping. You're telling the company, "Hey, I was really moved by your mission, and so I want to help." You begin building a collaborative partnership.

Part of the "dance" during the interview process for the C-suite is to learn as quickly as possible if you can be trusted to deliver on my promises. Successful partnerships are built on trust. For example, if you hire a junior engineer to handle a few tickets in the QA backlog, it is relatively easy to know whether those tickets were indeed closed out by looking at the backlog. There is a level of trust in the quality of the work, but the impact is minimal, and output is easy to measure.

If, on the other hand, you hire a VP of engineering, it becomes a lot harder to measure output since the consequences of their actions take longer to reveal themselves. You have to trust that the day-to-day actions will ultimately deliver the results you want from this person.

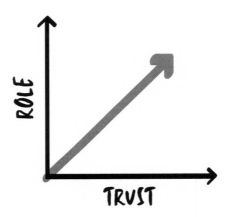

The longer it takes to reveal whether a decision is good or bad for the business, the more trust is required in the people making those decisions.

One could compensate for the absence of trust by building rules and procedures that don't necessarily require trust in people but have enough checks and balances to cover your bases in the event of missed expectations. For instance, keeping sprint cycles short, employing short-term contractual engagements, or outsourcing the same tasks in parallel to different companies will help the CEO build trust in your work.

Creating a solid collaboration relationship also depends on your ability to engage in small talk. Using the tips about reading body language from before, engage in small talk to help ideas and solutions flow.

I reflect back on a vicious cycle I got caught up in with the CEO at a relatively small SaaS company. I was CTO and in charge of product and was still coding to a small extent. He had a morning ritual of coming into my office to help kick off the day for both of us. I would usually be there already and immersed in my day. It was a bit of an interruption, but I grew to cherish it.

He would come into my office, sit on my couch, and start reflecting on his evening or how his week was going. This interaction helped push me past my facade and ever so gently coax me into the warm, fuzzy land where humans interact with each other. I enjoyed ideating and visualizing this way. When the timing seemed right to him during the conversation, he would lay his new ideas on me.

I vividly remember those conversations because they were like doing squats. In the first few, your brain is asking you why you're doing this to yourself. But you push through, and after those first four or five, your body settles in for the next ten to fifteen. There is an eerie quietness, as your brain isn't participating in any real conversation; it's mostly observing and reflecting back to you that you're going through the motions.

After this phase, the brain wakes up and protests the continuation of this ridiculous action. Remain focused, reading body language and engaging in small talk, as some people use this method of communication as a thin veil to work up to their ideas. Few people provide information only; most want to build a rapport with you.

You need to move through the small talk to get to the ideas. When there's true merit to an idea, you'll find yourself leaning in, making eye contact, and having an animated back-and-forth conversation. Before you know it, there will be a list of tasks and deadlines built to make the idea become reality.

Another part of collaboration is rewriting documents to make them yours. The CEO will have a ton of documents on value proposition, customer positioning, and so on, and you need to take ownership of those. Write the "why" of the document in your own words. Why does the document exist? What does it do for the company? Why are the policies in place? Are the policies updated and appropriate for the business? What steps are necessary to improve these documents and make them work for the business? Rewrite everything.

You need to poke holes in statements to make sure they are waterproof. If they aren't, it's your job to get the waterproof tape and apply the fix. I can't tell you how many times I was convinced I had some information, which I didn't write down, only to have it disappear on me later. Nothing is more important than to be able to demonstrate to your company that you understand the vision, the mission, and the values. The best way to gain this understanding is to write it down.

As you're rewriting documents, build flowcharts. You are probably the best flowcharter around because you already have years of logical thinking from product implementation or having to take complex problem sets and think through their logical steps. Draw up a few flowcharts before day 0 on the job to show how the product implementation would work or how it currently works.

Not only does this help you understand the company; it demonstrates to your future CEO that you have a handle on the situation. Again, you're still building trust. If you don't have access to the team, make sure that you have access to the product demo accounts so that you can draw out some flowcharts of how things work. While you will probably go through some of these exercises during the first few weeks on the job, don't underestimate the power behind opening up your brain through prep work of your own.

Being a part of the team even before you get the job will help you get the job. Learn everything you can about the company to build a better collaboration, including the finances. Brush up on Business Finance 101 because you'll be asking your new executive team to keep you in the loop on company finances. Look over the following terms as a beginning refresher:

Balance sheet. This is a financial statement that reports a company's assets and liabilities and shareholders' equity. It is a snapshot representing the state of a company's finances as of the date of its publication.

Profit and loss. There will be a profit and loss statement. This is a statement that summarizes the revenues, costs, and expenses incurred during a specified period, typically a fiscal quarter or year.

Cash flow. This is the net amount of cash and cash equivalents being transferred in and out of a business.

Budgets. These are estimations of revenue and expenses over a specified future period of time. Typically, each department will have its own.

Metrics. These are measures of quantitative assessment. They are commonly used for comparing and tracking performance or production.

BECOMING THE COMPANY CTO

Joining a new company is like starting a new relationship. You get to be the technology leader you always wanted to be. Starting as the CTO of a new company means that you'll have a new executive team, new direct reports, and a new company culture.

When you start with a new company, you will be introducing yourself to a lot of people in your first few weeks. You'll meet not only your new colleagues but also new and existing customers and investors. It is crucial that you get your introduction nailed down in month zero. This is the place to practice it so that it's perfect when you land that position. While it is imperative to remain professional among your network, mistakes at this stage are slightly more allowable. But get your introduction ready and practiced so you are prepared for an array of people in the corporate world.

Be prepared, as well, to help clarify with people what you do and why you're there. There is a misunderstanding with a lot of CEOs or CFOs that trickles down to their teams about what a CTO really does. By implication, the assumption is that we don't know how to manage people. That's why I think it's up to you as the candidate to come out of the gate with, "This is how it's going to work," and really coach the CEO on, "Hey, what do you need from me?"

This is what I'd like to do, typically. I'd like to record a quick CTO video on Friday afternoons, or I'd like to do a lunch and learn on Mondays. I think the more you come out and demystify to the C-suite how you're planning on managing and helping them grow, the more you're setting yourself up to succeed in 100 days.

I think an interesting aspect of the role of CTO is how you view yourself and how others view you. And I think the role of CTO has a particular disadvantage in this respect. Many times, the title of CTO will be given to someone when there's a lack of understanding, especially with first-time CEOs or a CEO who has no experience working with a CTO, where they think that *Okay, I'm the CEO, I'm building the business, and I need someone to build my tech.* The role of CTO gets conflated with the head geek or the leader of the development team. And while I do believe that the CTO should be superb at managing software delivery or has to be an expert at what it takes to deliver scalable, high-quality code to the organization, I really think that's just one-third of what is important or what makes a great CTO.

CEOs will often look at their CTOs as the implementers: "So, we'll do the strategy. We'll work on business goals and objectives. Our team will come up with quarterly goals, and then we'll tell the CTO what we need to have done." That's a problem, but it's an even worse problem when the CTO views themselves that way as well.

You must understand your desired outcome. Too often, we adopt a "wait and see" attitude. We look at what we have, and we see what we can build. What if we worked the other way around? I dislike hearing CTOs say, "I could only work with what I was given."

What if you built a team by reaching outside of what you were given? What if you created positions within the company to help the outcome? You have that power as CTO. Become resourceful and knowledgeable enough to know how to get what you need for your desired outcome. Throw out the old excuse "but I didn't have the resources." Find a way to get them.

While you're researching your best resources and the desired outcome that you will present to a company, research the domain in which you wish to engage. Look up as much as you can about the new company. Devour YouTube videos, read articles, visit the library, and do whatever you have to do to truly understand the business. You are trying to understand company goals, overall industry, company culture, and roadblocks to success for both the industry and the company, among other things. Dig deep into the company and their business to learn everything from every angle. This will drastically improve your confidence in brainstorming sessions but will also challenge some of the assumptions you may nurture when you walk into a new job.

I also recommend writing some code while you're working toward a new CTO position, even if you haven't done it in a while. It's a good idea to stay in practice. You'll accelerate your learning and ease the transition into the new job since you'll probably have to read through some GitHub READMEs and wrestle with some APIs. Don't forget to continue to work on yourself as well.

These personal actions are stepping stones toward building a great collaboration with CEOs in both the workplace and the consulting stage. When a CEO sees you as a partner, you are far more likely to get that salary you desire and the allowances you need to best improve the company.

RELAYING THE RIGHT PERSONAL MESSAGE

Who do you want to be and how do you want to show up to the role of the CTO? What do you have to do to be the best possible

CTO? Remember, your reputation will open doors for you, so you must make it shine.

It all starts with your values. Values are meant to be the guiding light when everything is dark around you. They are the set of principles that are foundational to how you respond in situations where your emotions have gone crazy and the world seems to be on fire.

I like to think of "values-based decisions" as decisions that may not make business or relational sense at the time but are 100 percent in accordance with your values. If I reflect on my years in various C-suites, there are traits that I have grown to love in a CTO. You'll definitely have your own, but if you need to get cracking on defining a set of values for yourself, I thought I'd list a few here that I think will serve you well in the C-suite.

Optimism

I think if you ask any CEO who's worked with CTO types, they probably won't use "optimistic" to describe their CTO's disposition. We are wired to think differently about the future. I love Paul Glen and Maria McManus's book *The Geek Leader's Handbook* because it gives a fantastic insight into how nontechnical leaders view the future versus how geeks see the future.

The authors describe how non-geeks see the future as promising, as clay that can be formed into something beautiful, and all it requires is imagination. Geeks view the future as looming; it is unknown and ambiguous. As "geeks," we need to plan for the worst and the extremes. How often do you start a statement with "Well, worst-case scenario…"? I know I do all the time. We've been trained to find the needles in the haystacks. For our mostly nontechnical CEOs, they find energy in ignoring potential obstacles. Negativity tends to follow, and they say, "All we can do is think about what won't work." This reminds me of how a CEO of mine once said, "It's my job to put the foot on the gas, and it's your job to put the foot on the brakes." How enlightened she was! It's important to be the voice in the meeting knowing what can and can't be done, or how long something will take, but if that voice has the undertones of pessimism, it's unattractive and shouldn't be heard at all, in my opinion.

It is possible to be the voice of reason *and* to be the optimist. We *can* be optimistic!

A mentor friend of mine, Aaron Contorer, once said we should "plan for optimism" as CTOs. Too often we design our systems around failure of the business or the plan, but how often do we think about scale and architecture in a wildly successful product environment?

We're constantly solving hard problems, often unnoticed. Let's remain an optimistic, positive voice in the C-suite.

Openness

This value has been a guiding light to me in the most difficult of circumstances, which is when I am misunderstood or when I feel unseen. Be open to feedback, points of view, misunderstandings, reexplaining, and everything you feel like you shouldn't have to be doing. This one is an ego-killer.

I was on a CTO engagement once where, after the honeymoon period, word in the corridor was that no one knew what I was actually doing. It was mostly a marketing company that wanted to capitalize on its success by creating products and more predictable revenue streams. I played a strong role in aligning the company with a technology strategy moving forward, and so I was really surprised at this negativity turned toward me. It cost me a few sleepless nights because I was very fond of the CEO and the company culture overall.

This is where I told myself to stay open. I reminded myself to not get defensive or offended. Just—stay—open. With purpose and determination, I engaged in conversations with the co-founders, COO, and key leaders in order to get feedback from them. My goal was to show them that I was open. I showed them that I took my role seriously and that if I was not in service to the team, then I needed to up my game. I had to show them that I was *ready* to up my game.

These conversations revealed a level of ignorance and self-importance, in my opinion, but that didn't matter. All that mattered was showing them what the role of CTO could do for them, for the company. Turns out they literally didn't know what the CTO role needed to accomplish, and that was a great reminder to be a proactive communicator. The corridor talk died down, and we got back to business.

A disposition of openness should not be confused with being the person everyone wants you to be. You're not open to having other people define the person who you are or the role that you're in. I say this because in my darkest moments, I get this confused. Remember who you are and show that to people, but do not bend to become something you're not. That will only lead to disaster.

Authenticity

If being open is essential to helping people around you see that you're teachable and ready to receive feedback, being authentic is a requirement. You are at your most authentic when your words and actions are congruent with your beliefs and values.

I believe that human beings are wired to sniff out inauthenticity. The easiest way to be inauthentic is to not do what you said you were going to do. How hard is that in the technology space? Let's say you promise, "This app will launch three months from now," and then it doesn't. "I'll get the architecture document on your desk by next week," and then you don't. A classic way to feed inauthenticity is to disappear. I mean, we know what we're doing. We're solving hard problems or dealing with unforeseen circumstances. But do they know it?

I'm a huge fan of Daniel Kahneman's work in *Thinking, Fast and Slow*. He talks about how it requires more energy for people to hold doubt in their minds than it does to slip into certainty. When your team starts doubting your authenticity, they will conclude that you are inauthentic. You've lost.

Be your authentic self. Have the confidence to let go of the person, the CTO, you think people want you to be. I promise you it will be more fun that way. Being stuck in the cycle of trying to please a CEO who can't ever be pleased will destroy you.

Transparency

Transparency helps me when I feel like I need to know every answer in every meeting. It also helps me when I am falling behind on promises I've made. Most of all, it helps me to be honest with myself. No secrets, no lies.

There is a process in our thinking that feels so visible to those around us but, in fact, is completely hidden. People have no idea how you've reached certain conclusions unless you explicitly tell them. They don't know how you're feeling, for the most part, unless you tell them. There is a construct of your persona in their brains, and it gets matched with reality with every touchpoint you have.

I love for those touchpoints to be my most transparent self, one where it is easy for those around me to perceive what I am thinking and they are free to observe me. Too often I want to be left alone to do my work, or I feel like it is too complicated to explain the technology process. I also feel sometimes that I'd rather let people into my big reveal than clue them in halfway for fear of unwanted feedback.

There might be merit to any of these situations, but they all contribute to an air of secrecy and the unknown. I want my job to be that of demystifying the technology process. My ego doesn't want to reveal just how easy some things are sometimes, but transparency demands that I let people in and include them in my process. You might be working against yourself to gain true transparency, but remember that it is all part of the process, and sometimes it's necessary to build an effective, collaborative work environment.

FIND YOUR OWN VALUES

It's time to find your own values. This will be essential in the coming months. It feels like a daunting task; I know it is a constant challenge for me. The thing is, you're already guided by your values; you just don't know how to put them into words. Here are my three *M*s for thinking about your values.

Mine. Values belong distinctly to me and do not exist so that I can please others. They give me a sense of value and self-respect. They are realistic and a true reflection of the person I want to be.

Mirror. My values are a mirror on my behavior. They help me see how I am acting when they are present and when they are not present.

Magical. I always feel a sense of wonder and awe when I think about the words that go into values. They should magically transform me from feeling weighed down to feeling inspired.

Look not only into your current life, but also your history to find your values. Where did you grow up? What were your family values? What mattered to you when you were in school? Can any of those values contribute to what you're trying to accomplish today? When values are solid, they last a lifetime, so look for those values that will still serve you now and in your future.

So after working hard in month zero, you've got the job, you're prepared for the first day, and you're excited, but be careful. It's not quite time to hit the ground running yet. You still have a lot of slow, careful work to do to ensure your first 100 days are a complete success.

PART TWO

100 DAYS BY THE TENS

5

YOUR GUIDE TO BECOMING A SUCCESSFUL CTO

Welcome to the first week of 100 days to CTO Excellence. You want to leave your mark and make a solid first impression. You may feel that you need to know all the answers right away. You don't. Double down on your past experience and reassure the CEO and executive team that they made the right choice in choosing you.

You may be tempted to hit hard with results, but I'm going to encourage you to take it easy this month. Utilize "thoughtful listening," also known as "listen and learn." Let's structure ourselves around succeeding both with the technology and with your team. It is important to remember that absolutely everything we do in our business leadership journey centers on relationships. Too often, we focus on business and hope that relationships will follow, when in fact, it needs to be the other way around. Relationships fuel business.

Understand that you are entering a system of "how things have always been done." Consider that if the system were working, you may not have been hired in the first place. But remember that people are set in their ways, and some may be resistant to change even though their current method isn't working. Your role will have a stereotype attached to it. If you don't demonstrate some sort of "win" early, you may become a victim of that stereotype. Remember you are your own uniquely wonderful person and not a stereotype.

You're going to need to learn as much as you can about everyone around you. You'll need to know who they are, how they interact with the team, their strengths, their weaknesses, and what they bring to the company. You'll have to learn how their expertise, skills, and habits help—or harm—the company overall.

This is the type of information you keep to yourself in a book of learnings that I like to call the CTO journal. This is a personal document that will become a reference book for your work with the company. You can use any writing app you choose. I use Google Docs. I prefer journaling electronically because it allows for easy copying and pasting or sharing, but if you have to do paper, then do it! Just make sure to use something that will easily help you expand because, as you move forward, you'll be adding to it regularly.

You're arming yourself with information from the beginning. You find yourself in the position to be the person asking all the questions other people are taking for granted, which will position you to be the person who knows everything. Begin this journey with intimate knowledge of the people around you.

Following is a breakdown of the first 100 days, divided into ten sections of ten business days each. At the end of every ten-day section, there are CTO journal exercises to help you implement the lessons and record your discoveries. These pages will guide you on your way to becoming a successful CTO.

6

DAYS 1–10: LEARN THE BUSINESS GOALS AND OBJECTIVES

WHY DOES THE COMPANY WANT TO USE THE TECHNOLOGY you've been hired to fix anyway? Understanding the business goals and objectives will answer this question for you. How will you make a piece of technology work better for the company if you don't know why the company does what it does in the first place?

Get user accounts for everything inside the company. No matter what it's for, get a user account and get inside it. Use every tool and figure out how each tool serves the goals of the company. Find out what subsets of each tool work best for the company and make notes in your CTO journal about tools that overlap each other. There's a template at the end of this chapter that you can use for this.

Some tools serve the same purpose as others, with small differences that make the company think they need both tools. This isn't always true. Dive into every tool to find these discrepancies.

Observe which team members prefer which tools and find out why. This will be part of your essential conversations. What aspects of the tools appeal to them? If the company is using different tools for similar tasks, ask why. You will save money and time by streamlining company tools, but first you must find out why multiple tools are in use in the first place. In fact, streamlining company tools might be your first month quick win (see "Identifying a Quick Win").

Make a list of projects that are currently running, and make sure that you immerse yourself in the work that's already been done. You'd be surprised sometimes that the conclusions you come to after weeks of deliberation may already have been documented before your time. There is always something to be learned from work that's been done before you, whether it's code, SOPs, or design documents.

Looking at what's been done before, what's currently being done, and what experiments to try for the future is a proven method. Consider Franklin D. Roosevelt and his action of bringing a brain trust with him into office. He made a statement with that action, and the statement was this: We are not pretending to know the grand plan to deal with the Great Depression. Instead, we are going to do a series of experiments and see what works and what doesn't. He brought enough experience with him to know that the problem did not have a grand, sweeping solution. Instead, it needed experimentation before a solution would be found.

Speaking from experience, as FDR proved, builds a sense of knowledge for those around you. In that first month, you work tirelessly to build up experiences as quickly as you can so you can grow in your voice of authority. A few ways to galvanize authority are experiences, data, and empathy. If you can speak for your customers, you can say, "I spoke to 150 customers, and I read the reports of the recent surveys you did. This is what we are hoping to accomplish on the larger business scale, and this is where we want you to have an impact on that."

USING YOUR STRENGTHS TO COMPANY ADVANTAGE

Yes, one of your strengths is in technology, but let's dive into strengths you probably don't know you have. Bring curiosity about the product and service with you. You already have that, don't you? If you didn't, you wouldn't have put in all that hard work and volunteer time before you got this job. Use that drive to research the company itself and find out how to make that product or service operate better as a whole, not just as a piece of technology.

That same curiosity will serve you in other areas of the business too. You've already signed up for all available services from the company, right? Use them. Find out how customers are buying and why. What, if anything, leads them to buy more from the company? If there is a free trial, what ushers the customer into purchasing at the trial's end? What's so great about the product or service? Develop your own empathy for the company's customer by going through the motions yourself. You'll gain a clearer picture of the company and understand why the customers do what they do. This is where you will see the start of the buying cycle.

Sometimes it requires many months to understand buying cycles. Do whatever you can do to try the product out in the meantime. If it's a mobile app that helps you get connected to your neighbors, then sign up and get connected with your neighbors. Use the app. Begin to understand why customers love the app or why they may be drifting away.

Look at customer reviews critically. What is the word on the street? What are customers saying about the product overall, and why are they saying it? Consider conducting market research with top customers for products with negative reviews to find out what customers really want and why they seem unhappy with the product. Ask customers what improvements would make them love the product more. Consider their answers and find ways to make them happen. Again, this might become a first-month quick win.

Finally, use your intelligence to your advantage. You didn't get here through luck alone. You worked hard through networking, volunteering, and impressing the right people with your expertise. Use that and build on it. Build relationships, have essential conversations to find problems, and document your ideas to help solve those problems. Continue to build on your CTO journal using the exercises at the end of each chapter because the journal will become your guide to moving around the company.

COMPANY ORGANIZATION

You will need to understand how the company is organized and who is in charge of what, both outside and inside their official titles. Record your observations. If you see anything that needs changing, whether it be low-hanging fruit or complex matters, jot it down in your CTO journal using the template at the end of this chapter.

A huge advantage of documenting your ideas is that some of your ideas may be unfinished or inaccurate as you base them on unfolding facts. Writing them down is *a lot* better than saying them out loud. You may inadvertently be making enemies or building unproductive alliances if you speak out too soon. Get the ideas on paper first. Sleep on it.

This documentation will be used for your goal setting and your quick win, discussed later. It will also be the foundation for the duration of the time you spend with the company. You will refer back to it, building on it and making appropriate changes to it as you get to know the company and the team better.

CTO JOURNAL EXERCISES: DAYS 1–10

1. Which subsets of each tool work best for each team? Use the template below to record your discoveries.

Team Tool Use

Name:

What tool are they using?

What are they using it for?

Is there a better tool for them to use?

Why are they currently using this tool?

How open do they seem to be to change?

1. Make a list of projects that are currently running, and list ways you could immerse yourself in the work that's already being done.

2. Try the product and look at customer reviews critically. Note your findings.

3. Record how the company is organized; who is in charge of what, outside and inside their official titles; and anything you see that needs to be changed.

Some ideas to consider journaling about include:

- Who stands out as leaders in the company? What do you like about them? What do you find challenging about them?

- Who do you like, and what do you dislike about them?

- Who do you find more challenging to be around, and what, in particular, do you find hard to navigate?

- Draw your own organizational chart of the company. Even if you've been handed one, make it your mission to draw one out for yourself.

- What are some of your early observations regarding improvements?

- List opportunities for improvement as you notice them.

Based on the list above, your CTO journal record might look like this:

Employee 1

Name:

Position:

Attributes:

Drawbacks:

(Repeat above for everyone)

Overall Company Layout

Who are the apparent leaders here, and why do I find them to be leaders?

Organizational Chart of Company

CEO:

CFO:

COO:

CIO:

Chief Human Resources:

Chief Supply Chain Management:

Other (fill in as needed):

Opportunities for Improvement:

7

DAYS 11–20:
LEARN TO SOCIALIZE

DALE CARNEGIE SAYS, IN HIS BOOK *HOW TO WIN FRIENDS AND Influence People,* "You can make more friends in two months by becoming interested in other people than you can in two years by trying to get other people interested in you."

Sit down with members of the team and talk. Get personal without oversharing. Get them to talk about things that are important to them. Practice active listening, where you rephrase what they say to you and repeat it back to them. Audibly and visibly show the person that you're listening. Maintain eye contact and don't look at other things while they're speaking.

If you'll indulge me, let's take a look at a typical conversation where you can have impact beyond the superficial. Take this conversation as an example of active listening:

Alice, CTO superstar: "Hey, Bob, how's it going today?"

Bob, COO superachiever: "It's alright, Alice. How about yourself?"

Alice, noticing a Gay Pride mug on the desk: "Hey, did you make it to the Gay Pride festival this weekend?"

Bob, visibly disappointed: "James and I go every year, but this year we never made it. His parents are in town, and they aren't exactly open to celebrating with us. It's been tough going for James and his parents ever since he came out."

Alice: "Ah, yes...I'm sorry to hear that. It has to be hard. I remember my dad having a really hard time when my sister came out. It took a while and a lot of support from us, but things finally seem better."

Bob: "Yes, we can only hope that things will get better for James and his parents."

Alice: "Well, I'm here for you if you ever need to chat."

Bob: "Thank you, Alice"

Throughout the conversation, Alice was looking directly at Bob. She glanced at the desk for only a brief moment to see the mug. She kept her hands away from her face. She leaned forward slightly in the chair and kept her feet on the floor. Her arms were at her sides with her hands on the armrests. Her facial expression appropriately reflected Bob's comments, from a slight smile when talking about the Pride festival to a slight frown and knowing nod of the head when discussing the tensions within the family.

Alice heard Bob, processed the information, and gave it back to him in a way that made Bob feel heard. The next time Bob and Alice meet, Bob will remember that Alice seemed to genuinely care about their conversation.

Your goal is to get that person to talk about themselves. The idea of small talk is to listen more than you speak and pose questions that inspire the person to communicate back ideas and concepts. Instead of hacking the person's response to find holes in their story, use the response to ask more questions that can communicate even larger ideas.

Small talk is your springboard into gaining not only trust, but a sense of intimacy with the other person. This intimacy is the foundation for future conversations that aren't as easy, such as the innermost workings of the company itself. People must feel secure with you if you hope to collaborate with them easily in the future.

Small talk can start with anything, from where they live, to how many kids they have, to what types of pets they like. Ask where they grew up. Ask what they did over the weekend. Use visual cues, such as that Pride mug, to start a conversation. When you ask these questions, you're trying to get them to open up and talk about themselves. We have an inherent desire to talk about ourselves, and it leaves us with a happy feeling when we feel someone else has heard what we've said. You are doing the small talking and the other person is doing the big talking.

Small talk is relationship building. You want to leave the impression that you're a good person. You want to build a sense of friendship. You want people to smile when they see you coming. It will help them become more open to collaboration with you. They will trust you and more readily follow your recommendations.

It doesn't happen all at once either. It is an ongoing process, even after the first month, or even the first year. You are building a professional relationship, and like all relationships, it must be maintained. Engaging in small talk on a daily basis is an important part of your job and often leads to more important topics.

Here are a few ideas to get you started on personal conversations:

- When did you join the company?

- How did you end up in this city? or Where are you from originally? (Yes, yes, these questions aren't all that bad. Plus, you gotta start somewhere.)

- What drew you to the company/idea?

- What do you love about our products or your current customers?

Remember to keep your tone light and conversational. This isn't an interrogation—it's a friendly exchange. Smile, make eye contact, nod your head, lean slightly forward, and use the other person's answers to support your next question or comment.

ESSENTIAL COMPANY CONVERSATIONS

This is where we go deeper into the conversations and learn how to move from small talk to the important discussions. There are building blocks to conversations. How can you move conversations about your kids to conversations about company issues? As you get to know people personally, you build a relationship that is the foundation for your professional journey.

I remember once when a COO with whom I had built a great relationship got mad at me. It's one thing when the CEO gets mad at you, but for me it's entirely different when the COO does. You're kinda supposed to be the same person, detail- and process-oriented.

About three months into a new CTO gig, I got a frantic call from our COO because a tool the VP of sales was trying to roll out wasn't working with a newly implemented system that yours truly introduced to the company. Clearly, she wasn't happy because the VP of sales wasn't happy, and they both wanted the issue resolved that day. I'd had a pretty good relationship with her up until then, so this was largely out of character for her. This bugged me, *a lot*.

The emotions I felt were a dark and stormy play on my ego. Firstly, why was the VP of sales "rolling out tools"? Secondly, why were they trying to integrate tools without consulting me? And thirdly, why was the COO undermining my authority as CTO?

I asked to talk to her, but she punted me over to the VP of sales. It was not a great conversation because he was new and was advocating for a process that worked for him from previous experiences, and I felt like he had escalated the situation.

I was able to explain to him why we should hold off on integrating the different tools, and I focused on the fact that the integration was a way of automating something before we had sufficient information about the process. I used "walk before we crawl," "eat our own dog food," and "before we automate, let's create"…but I felt like I was using clichés when, really, I was just angry. The call ended with us agreeing to reconvene the following week and to hold off on the integration. Crisis averted, right?

Absolutely not. The COO was pissed.

I was able to get her on a call, and I don't remember what I was thinking because I felt pretty agitated. I also knew that, as CTO, my head was filled with a ton of information that they didn't have, *but* the same was true for the other way around. I started the call with the intent of finding a way to communicate my thoughts in a way that she'd be receptive to. I was very much aware of the fact that as CTO I was in service to her, but I knew that we were very much in disagreement on how to move forward.

My conversation points went like this:

- I'm excited for the work we're doing and looking forward to our shared success as we roll out our systems.

- I would love to know more about the challenge you're facing and how I can support you in that.

At this point there was a shift because I realized she was under a lot of stress and super frustrated by an agreement she had with the CEO that I was totally unaware of. So the conversation shifted from me wondering how to enforce my CTO thinking on the process at hand to what I could learn from her.

This was a game changer.

I went from thinking that I had to navigate a delta between where she was and where I needed her to be, to *Hey wait, she knows stuff. What can I do to learn as much as I can from her?*

This kicked off a new principle for me, which was that everyone, absolutely everyone, has something to teach me. Learn what that is, ask them about it, and learn how to draw on each other. You're building a working foundation with positive interactions. This way, when the inevitable disagreement happens, you can lean on that positive foundation to resolve it.

What happens, though, when you meet people you don't like? It's inevitable that you will meet members of the team that you naturally don't vibe with. I personally struggle with people who have an inflated sense of importance or who assert their opinions. This may sound cheesy, but time and time again, the following reframe has worked for me:

- What strengths does this person have, and how have they brought the company this far?

- What weakness do you identify in them, and how is the company unaware of the fact that they're asking this person to do things they're simply not wired to do?

- What can you learn from this person? Name two or three things, but also perhaps things you've already learned from them.

- How can you show them that you see them and appreciate their strengths?

Write it all down in your CTO journal. Next time you're in a meeting with them and you feel like they're rubbing you the wrong way, recognize that this is your issue and yours alone, and then ask yourself, *How can I "yes, and" their ideas?*

The concept of "yes, and" attaches positive attributes to a negative situation. You're human; there are people who will rub you the wrong way. If you can find a positive in their ideas and say yes to it, you will effectively hide your disdain for him or her and help yourself build a positive relationship. Look at the idea itself instead of at the person presenting it.

Let's say a person is coming across as "better than you," a trait I've mentioned is a tough one for me. Take some time to really hear their idea and isolate that idea from the person. Take the idea apart inside your own mind, even if, as a whole, it's not a great idea, and find a place where you can say yes. Say "Yes, and we can add this attribute to that" instead of saying "No, but here's another idea." The language you use makes or breaks the conversation.

Remember that technical people tend to use language to transmit information. In fact, *The Geek Leader's Handbook* tells us that "too many of us think that communicating looks something like this:—gather data—list it in an email—hit send" That's it. Just the facts, ma'am. However, nontechnical people use language to communicate ideas and concepts.

What I find interesting, as a technical person, is that small talk is not transmitting information. It is communicating ideas. As someone who needs to participate in small talk, you're not trying to get information from someone when you use it. You're trying to build a relationship by discussing concepts and ideas. Practice this before you come into a company. It is a learned skill, but one that you can master over time.

ASSESSING EXPECTATIONS, BALANCING REALITY

By now, you've covered a lot of ground. However, it's important for you to remember your limitations. Keep your scope of work within a category of things that you can do. You have strengths; lean on them to show the CEO that hiring you was a smart move. Is there an enhancement to the product that can generate more revenue? Can you find a place to enhance the customer experience? Where is that quick win that will showcase your capabilities?

Stay away from staffing and hiring for now. It's easy to say, "Well, I'm going to fire this person." I would be cautious about making personnel changes right away. You haven't gotten to know people yet. Remember my argument with the COO? What was the end result? I came to realize that the issue was outside of how she did her job, and I was able to find a suitable solution. Walking in and firing people right away could backfire. You might find out later that the person you fired was one of the strongest assets to the company. Note that this doesn't mean you can't fire them later on. Wink wink.

Find out which ideas are most realistic by getting to know the people, the company, and the product through brainstorming sessions. You can facilitate a brainstorming session in a way that unlocks or breaks down walls between certain departments and ways of thinking. You can gather ideas, add to your CTO journal, and find issues as you look from outside the organization.

Again, remember that everyone here is close to the problem and may not see it because they live it. Brainstorming sessions are an opportunity to lay out ideas, find out who contributes to what, and get to know the company intimately. You have this power; it is one of your strengths. Use it to balance your expectations with the reality of what's happening within the company.

I would also stay away from calling brainstorming sessions that go too deep. As examples, value stream mapping exercises or threat modeling exercises could ask too much from people you don't yet know. These are incredibly valuable sessions to have, but they do require trust and a safe space. As an outsider, you may not yet have earned this trust. Facilitating meetings where people give an account of not only what they do, but also the inefficiencies they face in adjacent departments may have an outcome that's too hard to control.

Approach the company with a confident understanding of what you're doing and what your role is to give the company realistic expectations about you. They may have unrealistic expectations about what you will do for them; their aspirations for you might be too high. Help them by bringing them back to reality and discussing goals together.

I'm not saying it's always like that, but I think that the way your role might be perceived, because of past relationships, you may be pigeonholed into a stereotype about what your role needs to be. The first quick win you identify and accomplish will upset the apple cart a bit. It will show people the reality of what you are there to do.

Balance expectations with reality, for yourself and for the team.

In this chapter we spent some time focusing on your words—words as a means to connect with your colleagues. We love words that naturally bring people into a vulnerable space because this builds trust. We saw that this trust is the key to our working relationships being honest and fruitful. We also saw that the way in which we use words can set healthy boundaries and expectations for those who rely on us.

Coming up, we'll take a look at how to have our words met with action. After all, we know that actions speak louder than words.

CTO JOURNAL EXERCISES: DAYS 11–20

1. Who did you have personal conversations with in the last 10 days?

   a. Name:

   b. Main talking points:

   c. Name:

   d. Main talking points:

   e. Name:

   f. Main Talking points:

2. Who do you think you can learn something from?

   a. Name:

   b. Name:

   c. Name:

3. What three aspects about your role do you think will have the most impact on the people around you?

   a. Role:

   b. Impact:

   c. Role:

   d. Impact:

   e. Role:

   f. Impact:

8

DAYS 21–30: SET GOALS

AGAIN, IT'S IMPORTANT TO NOT COME OUT OF THE GATE running. Believe me when I tell you that if you accomplish outstanding goals right away, you will have nowhere left to go. Yes, you want a quick win right away, but you also want to take your time getting to know the company and the team. This is the time to take your time and learn as much as possible about your new surroundings while looking for your "quick win."

The "quick win" is an accomplishment you complete to show the CEO he or she made the right decision in choosing you, but it also buys you the time you need to dive deeper into the company itself. You must proceed with confidence and with a personable approach to gain access to everything throughout the company.

Use caution, however, because there is also the possibility that you might squander this time as a timid person who stays in the background. You don't want to set the bar too low for achieving goals, and you don't want to have a lukewarm approach. There's not enough time to do that. While you don't want to come out of the gate running, you don't want anyone saying, "What's that new guy do, anyway?"

This is why you want to create goals right away, even if you don't share those goals with other people. You want to look for that quick win that will eliminate any doubt that you should be there.

In my experience, the quick-win opportunity reveals itself in the most unexpected way. One time, I was brought on to CTO a company through a rough patch. They were struggling with monetizing their online course in a way that would create monthly recurring revenue instead of one-off purchases.

As we were grinding out late nights talking about future technologies and products that could fuel a subscription model, I noticed that they were really struggling with their learning platform. Changes would take forever, and course creators had to go through the technical team to upload content and make changes.

My quick win for the first month was presenting a plan for transitioning the courses from the old platform to a new one built for course creators. This win bought me incredible favor with almost everyone in the company.

While you are in information-gathering mode, you also want to watch out for information overload. There may be a lot of hope and expectations communicated to you in the beginning. Remember, they may be very excited to have hired you and then swamp you with all of their ideas.

Be careful with appearing like you've had an information over-load. Learn how to recognize the most important information and add it to your CTO journal. Be prepared to say no to certain meetings and to politely listen to ideas, making mental notes as to which ideas you will not be using. Remember that these are people who are close to the problems and, for that reason, may not be able to see the issues for what they are.

As you make your goals, avoid getting dragged into a system that won't allow for you to make innovative suggestions. Join brainstorming sessions and attend C-suite meetings. Ignore the comments that "The last CTO never came to strategic meetings," or "We always just did things this way, and we never had data for that."

You are not the past CTO or part of the past processes. You are present to help repair broken systems, both technological and interdepartmental. Remember that you have the knowledge; you've done the research. You have license to access whatever parts of the company will help you assess and fix it. Moving yourself into these meetings, learning about existing systems, and not worrying about the way things have "always been done" will help you identify that quick win and will help you accomplish it in an impressive time frame.

Before you can identify the quick win, however, there are things you need to understand. Learn who you can meet with right away. Find out who is open to brainstorming sessions. Learn to sit down and get to know the company on a human level. No one in the organization is too small or too big to meet with you and for you to get to know. You're setting the temperature of your time with the company right away. If you don't pay attention to this in the first 100 days, you're setting yourself up for failure.

For example, if you overcommit yourself in the first 100 days, you might fail miserably in the second 100 days. Make it your goal to find the balance between overcommitting and not delivering enough. Remember that delivery is essential in this industry. Pacing yourself over time is far more important than delivering a large "wow factor" straight out of the gate. Set a goal to get to know the company from its most important asset, its people, and then find a small, quick win that will solidify your place among them.

IDENTIFYING A QUICK WIN

The quick win is that improvement that has immediate benefit, is visible by the team, and can be delivered in the first month. It shouldn't be profound; in fact, making it too profound sets the bar too high for yourself. The stakeholders and C-suite have to agree that it's a good thing.

The thing that I think is critically important is identifying a quick win. Make your first goal all about the quick win. You're not seeking justification here; you're looking for a coaching moment. You're looking to educate the C-suite about your role as the CTO and what you will accomplish in that role. This will prepare them for what will come in your future as their CTO. You're setting the wheels in motion for your tenure. You're proving that you are not a normal CTO. You are an extraordinary one.

A lot of people will say that it takes three months before you understand anything. I would say instead of having the mindset of "I'm going to take it easy," instead say, "I want to demonstrate the value of the role of CTO as quickly as possible." This is how you will show your C-suite that you deliver value and why the quick win must deliver that value. Go back through your CTO journal, work through the list of opportunities you've identified, and ask yourself how you can best deliver something of value from that list. Show them they made the right decision hiring you, without going too far overboard.

Ways to identify a quick win include:

- Looking at the budget

- Looking at the software

- Looking at the product

- Looking at sales

- Using the product

- Using your knowledge of the industry to look at the product

- Using your knowledge of the competition to gauge the product

- Using your understanding of business systems to identify interdepartmental issues

- Using your understanding of the human element to recognize burnout within the company

- Brainstorming with the team

- Observing and listening to end users

- Analyzing support/trouble tickets

There is a lot to be said for identifying what this win might be for the company and then seeing if you can deliver on it. Being the new person, becoming one with the culture, and the pure nature of building technology products are all to your advantage. In other words, how do you show your C-suite or your peers at the new company that wow, this person who we just hired has already delivered a certain type of value. The purpose is to have them feel a certain way after interacting with you, and it's the quickest way to get them to feel a sense of trust.

BUILDING A QUICK WIN THROUGH EXPERIMENTATION

Getting that quick win isn't something that happens as soon as you walk through the door. You need to talk to the people, learn the company, and use the product to find it. You may need to experiment with a few different options before finding your surefire quick win.

An early win for you might be to figure out who seems to be stressed out and what the workload spread is and then redistribute it. I've walked into situations where the COO is completely overworked, and they look at you as their savior. Be sensitive and empathic to their current workload and to their stress levels.

You'll also look out for which relationships are under duress. This isn't a game of politics. Rather, you are a soothing balm when you're able to insert yourself in some conversations and stay out of others. Understanding this balance takes practice, but once you get it, you will gain the ability to make better connections between departments.

Perhaps you find that the leader of the sales team understands the product but doesn't fully understand why it is at its price point. Perhaps you find that the CEO isn't communicating well with the COO, causing a breakdown in ideas exchange. These are issues that are small enough to count as a quick win in the first month. Perhaps you call a meeting with the head of sales and the CEO to discuss that price point, allowing both to contribute ideas. Perhaps you arrange weekly Monday meetings between the CEO and the COO to go over business practices and plans for the rest of the week. Over time, you will be that soothing balm that heals issues that may have been going unnoticed by those closest to the problem.

Another way to find that quick win is through the product itself. It's important to eat your own dog food. If you aren't already using the product, use it. You know that people too close to a problem usually can't identify it. This puts you in the perfect spot to do it. The development team might not be aware of a user issue because they are too close to the product; your quick win might be finding it and discussing how it can be fixed. The sales team might not see a flaw in an upsell when it's glaringly obvious. You have the vision to find issues like these and fix them because you are the outsider. You have the fresh eyes that will recognize issues, even as you are still getting to know the team.

Keep in mind that many people won't know what you're there to do, so you'll have to pull double duty in the first few weeks. You'll have to look for the overall company problems while reinforcing others' confidence in you. I often look at the role of CTO as the person being asked to deliver on tech. I had a fascinating conversation with a mentor where they casually mentioned that very few people in the C-suite know what it is CTOs do.

Think about it; you can kinda wrap your head around what the CFO does, right? They need to take care of company financials. You probably know the terms *top-line revenue, balance sheet,* and *accounts payable.* It doesn't feel that hard to wrap your head around what they need to do to keep the company on the right side of fiscal discipline and health.

How about the CMO? Well, if you've built a company, or in any way understand how humans buy things, it has to do with getting a brand out there with a message that compels people to give the product a second look, right? I can go on with VP of sales, director of customer success, and even the CEO. These positions are well known in business culture.

But welcome to the blank looks on people's faces when you ask them about the CTO. "Uhhh, they need to make our tech stuff work," or "how about fix the printers," or "hey, the website is down." I'm being mildly facetious, of course, but I think the closest term that demystifies the software development process that is colloquially used by the C-suite, is perhaps the term *agile.*

I think this is why we go through such popular terms like *cloud, AI,* or *remote teams*—because C-suites around the world are conflating the vast landscape of technology and its products and services to the terms that seem easiest to understand.

Welcome to the world you're stepping into. No one knows what you actually do. How can you best help people understand what you do? Describe to them the value that you're going to deliver, and then deliver that value!

What types of deliveries can you make?

In the true spirit of leadership,
it is your job to help others be successful.

Here are some potential quick wins. Do not limit yourself to this list, however. Use it as a springboard for discovering quick wins within your unique organization:

- Improving inefficient procedures

- Recreating forms

- Removing unnecessary steps from processes

- Searching for discounts from suppliers

- Reducing "safety stock" (any stock sitting around "just in case of a shortage")

- Improving communication between departments and/or individuals

- Beginning to use features in software previously ignored

- Revamping trainings

- Reducing costs through parts submission

This chapter addressed one of my most favorite topics: how to secure a quick win. We have within us the ability to make an early impact on the company. But quick doesn't mean reckless. We can be pragmatic and thoughtful while also searching for the opportunities to make a difference.

For the next 10 days, we're going to deepen our relationship with the business so that our impact is long-lasting and memorable.

CTO JOURNAL EXERCISES: DAYS 21–30

1. What obvious problems do you see in the company right now? Also list potential solutions to these problems that will take less than 10 days to implement.

    a. Problem 1:

       Solution:

    b. Problem 2:

       Solution:

    c. Problem 3:

       Solution:

2. Write down your choice for a quick win for this company.

3. Write down how you would pitch your quick win to the C-suite.

4. Write down how you would pitch your quick win to your direct reports.

9

DAYS 31–40: RELATE PERSONAL VALUES TO COMPANY GOALS

You lined up your personal values when you were looking for a job. Chances are they already line up with the company values, but there's still more work to be done to make sure your values will help the company move forward.

The first step in aligning personal values with company goals is to assess your own values again, this time picking out the ones that work with the company. These are values that you want to hold true for your time at the company because there will come times when you question yourself. It's only natural that we question our work and wonder why we're doing what we're doing and how we're doing it. Understanding your personal values and aligning them with company goals will answer these questions naturally and help you keep going.

Begin by isolating the values you had coming into the company, the ones you identified during your preparation phase. What are they? Split a piece of paper into two vertical columns. Write down your values on the left side and try to prioritize them. Think about what you want to accomplish in life and how you want to do it.

Record the company goals you in your CTO journal (more on this journaling exercise at the end of this chapter). Write them down on the right side of the paper. Which company goals align with the values you brought with you? Where can you make adjustments to help the company move forward with their goals? You're not dismissing your values; instead, you're finding ways to help them align with what the company needs.

As you work out your personal relationship with the company goals, continue to get to know the intricacies of the company. Start reaching out to more people and working past the small talk of the first month. This is when you will really get into the company itself and learn how the people within the company interact with their industry. Grab a coffee or a quick lunch with a few key people to accomplish this.

Stick with what comes more naturally for you, and that is to hang out with the people with whom you feel a natural synergy. Go back to that CTO journal. Who did you mark down as people you are most likely to get along with? That's who you're targeting.

The lunch and coffee dates are for one purpose only: you're building a relationship. You're working to discover how your values align with the company goals by getting an intimate feel for those goals. Who better to help you understand the meaning behind these goals than the people who live them every day?

It's helpful to take a notebook in which you take notes of points of interest, or even open a new page in your CTO journal. You can discreetly take notes of the most important points. People will be more receptive to note-taking during these more in-depth conversations than they would have been during the small talk phase. In fact, taking notes shows them that you are not only listening, but marking down important points to review later. It appears more professional and shows that you are truly interested in the company.

Back when you were engaging in small talk, you asked questions and had an exchange. This time, take your time listening to the speaker. This is an opportunity to show your new colleagues the "light in your eyes" and that you're open and willing to communicate. Focus on your own body language, making eye contact and turning your body toward the person. Don't cross your arms or otherwise close off your body. You will get more information with an open posture and positive body language.

What if you become the person who people start confiding in? Since you're at the highest executive level in the company, you're probably going to be privy to a few conversations that might make you feel uncomfortable. For instance, the CEO might make a few disparaging remarks about the CFO or co-founder. This isn't healthy, but it's human.

It is tempting to agree with people's points of view at your own expense at this stage, and I think that's okay as long as doing so doesn't clash with codes of conduct or your own personal values. Try not to do it, though. Allow the person to continue talking while you maintain eye contact, then gently change the subject when he or she is finished. The other person gets the message that you are listening and you want to help, but you want to help in areas where you can. Certainly, interdepartmental strife is something you'll handle eventually, but avoid letting these conversations turn into gossip sessions.

At every single turn in my experience as a CTO, I have come to face this uncomfortable aspect. It comes with the territory of building relationships. In fact, if you did your job well in the first few weeks, people will feel a sense of safety with you. Walking into information about how one leader feels about another can be played out in two ways. Both ways have to do with your mindset.

Short-term mindset. You feel accepted, included, and approved! Why not? You were just informed by someone high up, perhaps the CEO, of the insider interpersonal workings of the company. With the short-term mindset, you'll see this as a win and participate in the conversation in a way that reinforces the person's views. This provides more comfort that you're "in" and could possibly win over more approval from the person. There are, however, a few things to consider with this mindset:

- Is the person having a bad day and simply venting on an issue with the fellow executive that might not be in play the next day?

- What happens when you run into the other executive? How will you be in integrity with that person?

- What credibility did you give away to participate in the conversation?

Long-term mindset. The conversation is uncomfortable because you're not participating or reinforcing the person's views. In fact, you're acting as the voice for that person, not to defend themselves, but to perhaps ask probing questions that could sway the person's perspective. You're excavating the true issue at hand, and that takes work. There won't be an immediate payoff in that you probably won't feel great when you walk away from that conversation. Here are a few things to consider with this mindset:

- If this person is comfortable with sharing this information about someone else with you, you'd better know that they may be talking to someone else about you.

- Sometimes venting is okay! Be the person that they can talk to, but understand that this is probably not the best time to give advice. Here's why: if they follow the advice, and things get worse, then you are the one to blame. I think of these situations as the pursuit of being "blameless." It's not that you're trying to be Switzerland by taking both sides; it's about drawing attention away from the subject of the person's ire and gently steering their gaze to look inward.

BUILDING FROM THE BUSINESS GOALS AND PRIORITIES

By now, you should have a deeper understanding of the business goals and priorities. It's time to start using them to build up the business. Remember that you're there to fix issues, for example, missing data.

So, as the CTO, you have the right to say, "I want us to log and catalog data so that by the time our salespeople or customer success people come to us with a request, we already have that data in hand." You demonstrate an understanding of the company's sales goals and a recognition of a problem: lack of data. You've used the company's goals—sales—to leverage yourself in insisting on data. It is far easier to get people on board with your goals when they are built from the company's goals and priorities.

With that comes the possibility of providing an outsider's perspective. You have the advantage of saying things such as, "You think you're making money because you think that users are attracted to this type of solution. But when I look at the numbers, I'm noticing that customers are actually looking for something else. You may be solving a different problem." Again, people who are too close to an issue will not see it for what it is.

As the CTO of a SaaS company I co-founded, I was shocked to learn one day that our VP of sales had instructed her sales team to not demo our product at all during the sales cycle. This was our flagship product, and our engineering team was perfecting it every day. What do you mean it wasn't being shown off at all? In my most immature self, I was quite upset.

After a few rounds in the boxing ring, I was the benefactor of the VP's patience and wisdom as she taught me a valuable lesson: customers don't always have the problems that we think they have, and the assumptions we make about their problems are almost always wrong.

The fact was that our customers were still subscribing to our product in great numbers. Our VP of sales was quite strategic.

Obviously, she knew what problems our customers were solving, and her solution wasn't to sell them on the bells and whistles of a tech product. Instead, she leveraged our technology as a means by which our customers could solve their biggest problems.

I often say that people in CTO positions have well-practiced, logical thinking. They have a good understanding of complexity and are good at deconstructing. They look at different components to systems to understand how they interact with each other. That's you, in this system. When you foster these abilities, paired with a strong understanding of company goals, you have an upper hand. Understanding these goals is part of your preparation stage and why it gets stronger in this time frame.

You need to start asking, "How does this business really work, and how has technology provided the business with a product or service?" Compare that to where they've told you they want to go and determine if their expectations are realistic. Again, it's part of your job to bring expectations down if they are too high by using direct data to prove your point. Their expectation of what you are going to deliver is going to have the impact on the revenues that they believe it's going to have.

As you prepare for your role, and while you are in your role, you are continuously asking yourself key questions about the technology. How does it fulfill the business goals? Is there other technology available that better fits the company? Are there solutions going unnoticed by the C-suite that you, as an outsider, see? How do you open up the C-suite to these solutions?

One of the ways to open people up is to begin in a place of wanting to support the company goals. When you lead with, "This solution will enhance this specific goal and help you get to that goal faster," your idea gets more attention. Your idea is heard more clearly and, often, is accepted faster.

More often than not, there are some unrealistic expectations. This is normal, especially since the people in the company are already close to the problem. They've tried to fix the issue to no avail; they've hired you to wave the magic wand. But you don't have a magic wand. What you have is a unique set of skills that will help you navigate through the problem and that will help you morph unrealistic expectations into fully logical solutions. Begin by understanding how to handle unrealistic expectations with the following tactics:

Manage Your Body, Manage Yourself

Imagine that the CEO comes up to you briskly and demands an answer to a question he asked you yesterday. You haven't had time to fully research it yet, and you don't have the answer. In that moment, you stiffen up and turn to fight-or-flight mode.

You have a few seconds while he talks at you to mentally calm yourself. Take brief stock of your body with an anchoring practice. For example, become conscious of your feet: press your heels into the floor as you remind yourself to breathe in and out slowly. You've "anchored" yourself to the floor to prepare a response. Really, what you've done is moved your focus elsewhere to clear your mind, so if focusing on a different part of the body works for you, do that instead.

Agree with the Principle

Remember that you and your CEO have joint goals for the company: success in whatever area is failing. The language you use at this point will guide the whole conversation.

Using the same example, say something such as, "Yes, I agree that I said I'd have those numbers for you. I will have them; I just have to run some metrics to get them. Meanwhile, may I show you what I've been working on today?" You've agreed that he needs the information, informed him why he can't have it yet, and then moved on to some realistically achievable goals.

Gauge the Interaction

Every person is different. Learn to read the person with unrealistic expectations and how to best bring those expectations into reality. Would it be better to behave proactively or reactively? The CEO above, with his aggressive, sometimes confrontational manner, probably needs a proactive approach. It's up to you to make the determination to help the team know what to expect.

From here, you can work on showing the team what to expect from you and when to expect it. As you gain more wins that align with the company goals, you will gain more favoritism around the office. People will begin to understand that you may not accomplish a goal right away, but you constantly have the wheels in motion to accomplish everything in a way that works best for the company.

GAINING A DEEPER UNDERSTANDING OF COMPANY METRICS

ESSENTIAL METRICS

FOR ALL TECH COMPANIES:
- REVENUE GROWTH RATE (RGR)
- CUSTOMER ACQUISITION COSTS (CAC)

FOR STARTUP TECH:
- BURN RATE

FOR SUBSCRIPTION-BASED BUSINESSES.
- CUSTOMER RETENTION RATE (CRR)
- LIFETIME VALUE OF CUSTOMERS (LTV)
- ANNUAL RECURRING REVENUE (ARR) OR
- MONTHLY RECURRING REVENUE (MRR)
- CUSTOMER EXPERIENCE

SPECIFIC TO HARDWARE COMPANIES:
- MANUFACTURING COST PER UNIT
- GROSS PROFIT MARGIN
- HARDWARE FAILURE RATES

Since you've gained access to most of the organization's data, you have access to the metrics. How are sales? How is the website doing? Is it serving the company as it should? How is the social media presence? Could it be stronger? What apps is the company using that are either out of date or do not serve the company as they should?

What is the revenue growth rate (RGR)? Is there a high customer acquisition cost (CAC)? Is everyone using the same technology, or is the CEO still on Outlook, while the rest of the company has switched to Gmail? These inconsistencies may seem small, but when they are switched to a streamlined system, the company overall begins to run smoother.

As you prepared yourself to work with this company, you researched how the company came up with their revenue model. You know how many people are subscribing to it, some general metrics, and how customers engage in general with the business.

However, you need to dig deeper into these metrics as you learn more about the company. How do the metrics interact with each other? How are key players in the company reading the data? Are they reading the data at all? Is the data available essential to the business, and is it aligned with business goals? As you know, companies have access to a lot of different types of data, but is your company using the right data the right way?

Sometimes there is a disconnect between the company and the metrics. Maybe the company isn't reading the data correctly, is reading the wrong data, or simply doesn't have access to the type of data that will help them operate better. This is where you step in with your deep understanding of the metrics and suggest ways to make the data work for the company.

You're using the access to the inner workings of the company that you were granted before to look at the bigger picture. You're also using your outside knowledge of different types of data to impact the company. Your C-suite might not know they're using the wrong data set to answer their questions, but you know, and you know which data set would work better.

You're also using this opportunity to make sure the existing technology is presenting the correct metrics. For example, is the marketing department using an outdated piece of software to figure out customer acquisition cost? Is there a breakdown in the subscription service that is reducing the customer retention rate, and where is the breakdown? What technologies can be implemented, changed, or possibly removed to help improve the company metrics?

There's a beauty in company metrics that not everyone is lucky enough to see. Merely numbers, they reveal everything from financial changes to interdepartmental problems.

Let's say you've looked at the manufacturing cost per unit for the past eight quarters, and you notice an anomaly in the margin due to a slight upward spiral. You've done your homework and see that the costing data has been masked by an unusual corresponding increase in sales. Yes, sales are going up, but the cost to produce one product is also sneaking up. What's causing the increased cost in production, and how can the company best protect themselves against a disaster if sales suddenly take a sharp decline?

You have to get intimate with the metrics. You have to let them become your best friend. You have to get so comfortable with them that you dream about them. If talking to people and building relationships is the frame of the company, the metrics are the concrete. They hold up the company, and any cracks must be repaired to help the company stay strong.

We learned in this chapter that, as with all things, understanding our environment starts with understanding ourselves. What we bring to our company is rooted in our personal values, and it requires effort to marry that with the company culture. But we also saw great gains to be made when we are able to measure our company's progress toward the goals set by the leadership team.

Next up, we'll take a look at the importance of our voice inside the company.

CTO JOURNAL EXERCISES: DAYS 31–40

1. Who did you have coffee/lunch with?

2. What did you learn from each of them?

3. What are the business objectives for this company for this year?

4. What are the business objectives for the company for next year?

5. Write down the top metrics by which the progress toward business objectives is measured.

10

DAYS 41–50: UNDERSTAND COMPANY DYNAMICS

COMPANY DYNAMICS IS MORE THAN WHO IS IN WHAT ROLE. Humans interact with each other, and this is all part of the human metrics. Who does the CMO talk to the most? Is it the head of sales? Perhaps it's the head of engineering. Why does the CMO talk to that person more than others? What problems exist that drive each individual company relationship?

Scratching the surface of who talks to whom, and why, uncovers problems that are just waiting to be solved. You are the person who will solve them. Lean on plausible deniability during this month as you learn more about the overall human metrics.

Plausible deniability at this stage is you saying, "Oh, I wasn't aware of that policy," or "I didn't realize those two people were close friends outside work." It allows you to get deeper information, especially as you work toward aligning your values with the company's goals. How else will you line these things up if you can't get deeper information?

Let's say, for example, that customers are leaving the company because of bugs in the software. Here's the thing: if technology is viewed as an impediment to success, then that technology will be resisted. What if the technology isn't the issue, though?

You need to be on your defenses when it comes to interactions involving the real issues behind the superficial problems. For example, let's say that a bug in the software used by the employees exists, but no one has told the engineering team about it. They just stopped using the technology, when it is actually a technology that would better serve the company.

What caused that breakdown in communication? Here you are, looking from the outside, ready to uncover the real issue behind this lack of communication. Perhaps the head of engineering is unapproachable. Perhaps the C-suite is too overwhelmed with other issues and decided that this bug was low priority.

Whatever it is, you want to address it to help the C-suite become more successful as a team. And if you can come in as CTO and communicate a vibe that you want people in the C-suite to be successful, you will gain bigger wins.

BECOME A CHEERLEADER

Your weeks should be filled with phrases like "That's awesome, Sally," or "I really like that idea, Andrew," or "How do you think we should approach that?" Your role as CTO is to bring the best out of people. It doesn't mean you're placating, but rather that you're looking for opportunities to identify valuable work and the person behind that work. Notice how I'm not thinking about ways to improve or consolidate or help. We are looking for ways in which we can build foundations so that when times get harder and tougher decisions need to be implemented, you have the understanding and support of those you need most.

This is a great time to evaluate how much you've listened versus spoken versus. let others speak. It is so tempting to constantly use words to show the team that you're valuable. Yes, teams love to laugh, and it's tempting to measure our value in how much we can make our teams respond favorably to our points of view or our jokes, but at the core, we don't need a group's buy-in; we need individuals to feel valued, respected, and heard.

What better way than to let them convey their knowledge on a subject, which gives them an opportunity to shine?

I know your personality type feels valued by the ideas you can generate. Imagine how hard it is for me to shut my mouth when someone else communicates the ideas I shared with them? But I can tell you, almost every time I took the mantle from them, it left a bad taste in my mouth.

Let them have the idea, because you are there for support. You are using your expertise to build up the company so it will eventually run on its own, built on the foundation you helped to develop. Sometimes you may have to let someone else claim your idea, but you do so because you're keeping the big picture in mind.

Let's say you suggest that the CEO use a new email service to streamline communication for the sales team because that service allows the head of sales to forward important information to the sales team in a more efficient and secure manner. The next time you're in a meeting with everyone, the CEO announces, "We will be using a new email server, so please look for instructions for switching in the next week." He forgets to mention that it was your idea. That's okay because you're fixing the big picture. You're supporting the CEO and how he manages his people by staying quiet after the announcement.

Generally, people know where ideas are coming from and that changes happened after you showed up. You will be given credit for fixing the overall picture, even if you have to let go of credit for some small ideas along the way. You're giving away small battles to win the war.

Be a cheerleader and the person behind the scenes who provides support to the team. Let go of ideas when necessary, and encourage people to keep going. Acknowledge the great ideas, and be as positive as possible to everyone. Even when you have to shoot down an idea, do it in a way that makes the other person feel that they still have control, that you are merely offering a suggestion.

It is even possible to remain a cheerleader when you have to shoot down an idea completely. When you hear something that you know won't work at all, use your knowledge of that person and his or her expertise to suggest something else. For example, you can say something like "I hear your idea, but what about the idea you had last week? Have we explored it thoroughly?" or "I understand the basis of that idea, but what if we used this other method within your expertise to create a new idea?" Show the person you support their free thinking and their dedication to the issue, while simultaneously trying to come up with the best solution together.

HEADING OFF THE EAGER BEAVERS

What do you say when someone approaches you and asks eagerly, "Can you tell us your plan? What are you doing about this or that issue?" but you're not ready to reveal your ideas yet? I tell them that I'm still researching a couple things about it or that I'm not quite ready to present it yet. I'm almost ready, but there's just not enough research done to present a solid idea yet.

That has served me well because I avoid walking into a trap where half-baked ideas or unprepared assessments lead to unwanted conclusions or commitments. Telling excited folks that I'm not ready yet also shows that there's thoughtfulness in the process and that the idea will be communicated in a week or two.

It also gives them a shot of instant gratification to know that the CTO is thinking about the problem. It's like when you buy that gym membership—there's the instant gratification of being a member of a gym and feeling like you're doing something positive.

On the other hand, their insistence on an answer keeps me on a timeline, which prevents me from spending too much time on something or overthinking it. People are waiting; there's no time to overthink. In this manner, I appreciate when people ask for answers, as it also holds me accountable.

Let's say, for example, that you are trying to run some recurring revenue projections for a new feature you're about to release. The CEO knows this and is excited to see your results. After a week of waiting, she asks you for the projections. You're not ready.

In response, you can say, "Well, after my initial research, I see that I need to know the net sales from the last four quarters aggregated over our five largest customers in our system." With this answer, you're giving both an account for the work you've done as well as an update on what still needs to be accomplished.

I highly recommend that you not fall into the trap of on-the-spot thinking, on-the-spot planning, on-the-spot strategy, or lazy thinking. I think there's a time and place for open-ended brainstorming, and I'm not saying you should always tell someone "it depends" or "I can't possibly tell you the answer right now." I'm not saying you should be a robot that needs more input before you can respond.

I am just saying that I have seen too often the temptation that we have to respond to demonstrate our value, and I'm saying you should learn how to deflect in an authentic way that gives someone just a little hit. Then go and do the hard work of thinking through this. When you come back, you own the frame, you own the knowledge, and you are the one that is the authority versus being caught in an interrogation.

Sometimes, with the CEO, we think we have to provide a comprehensive answer to a question because that's what we, as CTOs, would expect from someone. That's not necessarily true. I know a lot of times, as CTOs, when we talk to people, we're asking ourselves, "Can I trust this person, and is this person smart enough to be telling me what they're telling me?" We're mentally analyzing the information as we receive it.

It's important to remember that the CEO may not think this way. He or she may want a fast answer; that simple hit may be enough for them. Perhaps the CEO merely wants to know you're working on the issue. When you say, "I'm still researching that," it tells your CEO that you are focused on the issue and you aren't just wasting his or her time and money. It's a bit of a dopamine hit.

Putting people off isn't a long-term strategy; of course, there must be results. But you still want to provide that little dopamine hit. I'm not saying you should be disingenuous. I'm saying you're not giving them all they want, but you're giving them the satisfaction that this is on your mind and you are thinking about this.

As you field these questions and do your best to answer everyone all day long, avoid lazy thinking. This is when someone asks you a question and you use your answer as an opportunity to verbally process your unfinished thoughts.

An example, and one I have faced more often than not, is the question of data science, blockchain, or artificial intelligence. For example, your CEO may say, "Hey Etienne, what are your thoughts on the future of AI, and how do you think it impacts our product line?" This is a problem because these are very big ideas and concepts, and in many cases, I hadn't thought about the impact to the company. There's a wide-open gap for rambling, for lazy thinking. Don't do that.

It might feel like a fun conversation in the moment, but in your capacity as CTO and in this field of expertise, you're expected to know the answers. If you don't have them, don't employ lazy thinking. It's always better to allow yourself time to build a clear, concise answer than it is to get caught up in idle pontification.

Lazy thinking says, "I have interesting concepts that I believe to be true, but I haven't thought about the implications if they were to, in fact, be true, so I am going to throw it out there. I am going to put something out on the table, and I'm going to see what the group says about that." You're basically going to facilitate your thinking, and, to me, there's a time and place for brainstorming and saying, "I don't know what the answers are, but, hey, I want to just throw this out there. Let's have a brainstorm session." This is not that place.

If lazy thinking is left unchecked, it becomes a strategy for "I'm really good at thinking on my feet. I know that there are certain things that are true in this universe." So then you use the time to color in the gaps, and then that coloring becomes messy.

I think that the best way to combat lazy thinking is to write stuff down to help your brain interact with the words as your fingers move to type those thoughts. You close the loop with your own brain versus inviting someone into it and trying to close the loop with another brain. Get the research done, and make sure things are sorted yourself while politely putting off the eager beavers and avoiding lazy thinking by not letting go of information before it is ready.

Giving a rapid-fire answer that leads to lazy thinking often happens when we lead through talking. On the C-suite level, there is a lot of talking. There are planned brainstorming sessions. There are sync-up sessions, random phone calls, ad hoc meetings, and more.

If you allow it, you can let yourself start getting sucked into situations that invite lazy thinking, especially if you're easy to be around or collaborate well. You find yourself pulled into someone else's verbal processing vortex. The conversation could be as innocuous as someone having a bad day all the way up to people really not knowing how to solve a certain problem.

HAVING MEANINGFUL CONVERSATIONS

Knowing how to ask the right questions, at the right time, is a honed skill that requires practice. In our best selves as CTOs, we're coaching, and in our worst selves, we're interrogating. When the CEO asks us a specific question, sometimes we jump straight into the hippopotamus's open mouth because that's what we expect from ourselves. Somehow, we think, *For me to answer that question, I need to build a whole narrative, say a certain thing, or act a certain way.*

If you tell anything but the truth about your timelines, or add too much information, you're creating false expectations. You wind up saying something you'll have to defend later. I don't think you're instilling confidence by over-answering questions, so when a CEO asks you, "When will that be done?" you don't have to give huge, never-ending answers. There's nothing wrong with giving brief, honest answers about your work in progress.

There's nothing wrong with throwing out a nugget and saying, "I actually have quite a bit to process with you on that. I've got some good news," or "I've got some concerns around that. Can we schedule some time where I can talk you through this in two or three days?" The negotiation now is around finding a time to discuss the project with the CEO. Another way to phrase it is, "You know what? There are actually two or three things I did want to run by you on this. It'll take me about thirty-five, forty minutes, so how about we go have coffee in two or three days? I'll take you out for coffee, and I'll run these things by you."

In its most simplistic form, you're buying yourself some time, but in a shrewder way, you're giving yourself some breathing room to be thoughtful about what you want to present. It's not just what you say but when you say it. Oftentimes, that short answer is all they want.

So you've set up a meeting time to have a meaningful conversation, but how should you go about it? These conversations could be a constraint for the CTO. I say this because in many cases, the CTO is more analytical and introverted. In other cases, more technical and skeptical. This could lead to awkward conversations.

Remember, this is not an interview; it's a conversation. We are not considering the CEO's intellect or assigning respect based on their skills of logical deduction. We're looking at them as a human being and remembering that they are in this role because of who they are. We're valuing their humanness over their skills or their competence. Follow these steps to prepare for a conversation that delivers value and results.

Do your homework. Of course you've been researching everything, from company metrics to possible solutions to issues. Have that ready when you arrive at the meeting. Bring your notes, your resources, and anything else you need to back up your ideas. If you need more information, bring questions that will help you get it. Being prepared further shows the other person that you are dedicated to solid solutions.

Show confidence. This is a must. Always show confidence and that you believe you should be there. You know things the other person doesn't—you're in the dregs of the business. You have that outsider eye that helps you see things others simply can't. Maintain eye contact; speak clearly. Smile and avoid backpedaling. Use phrases such as "That's a great point. Let me mark that for further research," and then make sure to write the idea down.

Establish context. Right away, tell the other person why you called this meeting. You both have a general idea, but what exactly do you need from him or her during this session? Do you need some information to help build an idea? Do you need access to something to help you with your research? Why are you here? Present your needs up front and make sure to acknowledge his or her needs.

Stay tight and focused. You may have a lot of information to share in a short half hour. Keep the conversation streamlined and focused on the topic. Get in and get out. Share your idea. Help the other person understand why he or she should care about it and how it is relevant. Discuss what you want the other person to do, think, or know by the end of the conversation. Write down bullet points if it helps, but keep the conversation on track to make sure you cover everything you need in a short time.

During these conversations, remember the emotional quadrant chart. The four sections are self-awareness, social awareness, self-management, and social management. Each of these quadrants can be applied to how to communicate meaningfully. Working on these four skills will support you in having these important conversations.

Always remember that emotion is quicker than logic—you will be faster to respond emotionally than logically to situations. However, using the four quadrants of emotional intelligence in the workplace will help you learn how to have even the toughest conversations.

Self-awareness, or what I know. You know a lot. You've done your research; you've taken the necessary time to get to know the company intimately. However, be aware that revealing how much you know too fast might be seen as arrogance. Sometimes it's better to let other people lead while you hold back some of your knowledge. For example, let's say that you're talking to an engineer. He's telling you all about a program he uses and how important it is to the company overall. You know it's important, and you already have a plan to make it better, in turn making his job better.

However, staying quiet and letting him talk it out is better than asserting your knowledge. You are aware that silence is better during this conversation because you have a firm grasp on social awareness.

Social awareness, or what others know and how they react to us. This one is a tough one, but it comes with practice. It's about understanding when to pull back and let others "reveal" their knowledge to you. It's about reading body language and learning when you might have said too much or talked for too long. It's about recognizing the subtle things people show us that let us know how the conversation is going.

Body language is a giant "tell" for the pulse of the conversation and is communicated without words. Is the person smiling, leaning toward you, and looking you in the eye? Great! She's engaged and wants to hear more. Is the person looking away, glancing over your shoulder, leaning back, or crossing her arms? Uh-oh. There's somewhere else she'd rather be. Tie up conversations when you notice this type of body language by suggesting revisiting the issue later.

Self-management, or what I do. Knowing when to tie up the conversation, and then actually doing it, is part of self-management and is highly effective in conversation. When you notice someone "checking out," make the decision to give him or her an out. You are showing compassion to the other person, and you are proving that you pay attention.

An "out" also works when you're asking for something that isn't essential to your job. For example, if you want to talk to the CMO about implementing a new social media technology, send an email saying,

> Hello Sarah! I have a new idea for an app that will help you reach more people on social media. Do you have time for a quick coffee tomorrow? I am also free Friday!

Giving two options for meetings gives Sarah that "out" that she needs to turn down one of the time slots without feeling that she's putting you off. Giving people outs leads straight into social management.

Social management, or what we do together. This is how you handle your relationships with everyone around you. There will be people you don't like, as I mentioned before. There will be a range of personalities, even in small companies. You, as the person who works with everyone, will need to learn how to have conversations with all of them.

Some people need time to talk about themselves before fully embracing a conversation about work. Others will walk up to you, fire facts at you, expect nothing but facts in return, and walk away, never even saying hello. You must learn who prefers which type of conversation and learn to communicate with all.

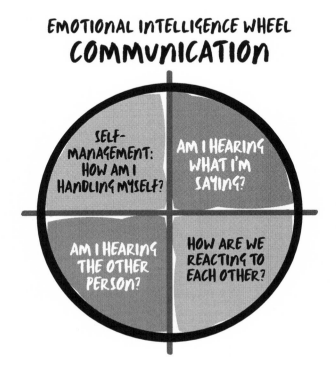

EMOTIONAL INTELLIGENCE WHEEL
COMMUNICATION

SELF-MANAGEMENT: HOW AM I HANDLING MYSELF?

AM I HEARING WHAT I'M SAYING?

AM I HEARING THE OTHER PERSON?

HOW ARE WE REACTING TO EACH OTHER?

Another word that is used to understand social awareness is *empathy*. Are you able to put yourself in the other person's shoes? Let's say I'm at the whiteboard and I'm drawing circles, trying to communicate something. Can I put myself in the chief sales officer's shoes and know that she is getting it? Would I understand what I am saying if I were her? The ability to take yourself out of your world and move into someone else's gives you a chance to see what they are going through.

Your job isn't only about emotional intelligence, but this concept plays a part in your success. It contributes heavily to essential conversations and how you go about asking the right questions at the right time.

Oftentimes, the CTO says the right thing at the wrong time or cannot read signals from other people. This is where a bit of the cliché behind the IT person comes into play. That's why studying and learning emotional intelligence is so important. That's why practicing what we learn in this area is so important.

We won't get it right the first time, but we will improve over time. When you make a mistake or miss a signal, evaluate the situation, find key takeaways, and move on. For example, your CEO, Kevin, asks you for an update on the promise you made in yesterday's meeting. Right away, you begin explaining your research in detail to him, assuming he wants all the details. He tries to maintain eye contact with you, but before long, he's looking at his watch and staring over your shoulder. Suddenly Kevin says, "I have a meeting to get to. Update me later?"

You wonder why you've been abruptly cut off, but you missed his subtle body language cues. This is an opportunity for you to reflect and learn in the areas of emotional intelligence for communication.

Finally, remember that you are on a fact-finding mission. You're not there to start or perpetuate gossip. Be careful in saying certain things. For example, if you're talking to the VP of sales, don't say, "Oh, the marketing person said that they haven't been able to see the pipeline in years." Don't be an antagonist, even accidentally. Avoid saying things like this altogether.

Instead, add them to your CTO journal to make sure you have a record of the contradiction. When you're in front of that VP, though, mention nothing about what someone else has told you. You have the ability to position yourself for collaboration. You become a facilitator of conversations built to fix this issue. When it's time for you to start making changes, you'll find yourself in a much better place to do so.

To circle back, remember that at your best, you are a coach. Be at your best while avoiding your worst, an interrogator. Let the other person lead the conversation. Learn how to read body language. Ask leading questions, such as "Explain to me how this is done. Then what happens? What is your process for this?" Give the spotlight to the other person and allow him or her to shine. As they talk, learn. Understand what you can about the organization through them.

We saw in this chapter how powerful our voice can be inside a company. We also saw that we should use that voice to be optimistic and attractive to our colleagues so as to always point them to the North Star. When we start to speak up, we also attract naysayers and doubters. We learned that this is nothing to worry about because through the power of meaningful conversations, we build up our reputation as leaders.

We are now at a place where we start to assert ourselves. This is the perfect opportunity to start steering the ship in the direction that you want it to go. Let's take a look at how to introduce your strategy.

CTO JOURNAL EXERCISES: DAYS 41–50

1. Who did you have meaningful conversations with in the last 10 days?

2. Describe how you acted on the four quadrants of emotional intelligence in the past few days:

   a. Self-awareness:

   b. Social awareness:

   c. Self-management:

   d. Social management:

11

DAYS 51–60: USE FLOWCHARTS AND DOCUMENTATION

Congratulations! You are halfway through your 100 days to CTO Excellence! How is it going for you? Have you noticed any change? Perhaps you're getting comments about the impact the new you is having?

Keep going! The next 50 days will be crucial in navigating tough situations. But you'll also find that you get to live out your love for technology and problem-solving on top of the platform you worked so hard to establish over the last 50 days. We will take a look at more nuanced issues that may arise and also make sure that your well-being is taken care of. You've got this!

At times, we connect with someone in a conversation and communicate certain things, but we are not understood completely. We think we've been understood, but the other person just hasn't fully grasped our idea. You might walk away from the conversation or meeting thinking that you've communicated your strategy, ideas, or plan, but that's not what happened. Even if someone is taking notes, there is tremendous value in making sure you are talking around a physical document and not just ideas or concepts that have to be reexplained.

Up to this point, you've been building plenty of documentation. Perhaps your documentation has been restricted to your CTO journal; perhaps it is more professional because you realized the company needed better written guidance. Whatever documentation you've created has the potential to become a sharable, tangible tool for your team.

Together with the presentation you created for your strategy, you'll need to begin creating visuals, especially for nontechnical people. People need something they can touch and spend time with on an individual basis.

What if your CMO is having a terrible day? His dog died last night, his kids are stressed, and his wife is mad because he came to work today because he knew he couldn't miss a meeting you've planned. He's here physically, but he's not absorbing everything you're communicating in the best possible way.

When you hand him a copy of your presentation or present him with easy-to-read charts, he has a chance to consume the information at his leisure to make sure he's absorbed it correctly. Since you don't know how people are absorbing your information, or even that they are, get used to presenting documentation to go with your official meetings.

As a CTO, you should be a prolific creator of documents that people can read. I had a great conversation with someone recently where we talked about how the completion of ideas is a thing. It's an action that you've taken, you've completed. You've taken the effort to think through the outcome of what you're planning or suggesting the company does before you've included people in that, so it's also a complete versus incomplete mindset.

Do you want to go into meetings and be surprised because a lot of your thoughts or ideas or premises, or whatever you're advocating, are just incomplete thoughts? Or do you want to go into meetings or strategies and demonstrate to your audience that this is a painting you've worked on for a long time and that people can see that?

I was the CTO of a company whose core product was people interacting with video, and the owners didn't know how long people were engaging. They literally did not know certain key aspects to how people were interacting with their product.

And so, as CTO, I jumped in and immediately started building dashboards and queried the database. I didn't ask my team to do it; I jumped in, and I put some dashboards and bar graphs in place to just give the founders a sense of *wow*.

I did this by using key metrics for the company. And so, if you're in the preparation phase, you need to know what the customer acquisition cost is and you need to know what the churn is, which is the rate at which people are leaving. You need to understand the net new revenues, and you need to understand customer lifetime value. And when you walk into the position understanding the business and you can marry that with the technology, where it is and where it needs to go, you become an incredibly important person in the C-suite.

While the written document is useful and helps communicate many ideas, flowcharts are natural for CTOs. We communicate in flowcharts all day, every day. It's an easy way for us to think. When you were mapping the business process in month one, you were mapping business goals and objectives to how technology comes full circle—you've already drawn that out for yourself.

Expand into other areas to get a fuller visual of the company overall. A simple place to start is with the customers. How do they get onboarded with the company's current system? Or you might describe the sales funnel specific to that company. Begin with an easy flowchart to build your way up to more complicated documentation.

Remember the flowchart in your CTO journal where you documented the major players in the company? Keep going with that chart. Expand it into squares as you learn more about the company and the employees themselves. Plot the business as a whole into squares that interconnect with each other to give yourself an overall breakdown of how the company operates.

I see this as providing a service to the company. This type of documentation comes from a service mindset because these flowcharts might be helpful in the future. This documentation, though, goes in your CTO journal. This is not something you'll be presenting to the rest of the company. It is a tool that helps you learn about the inner workings of the company and helps you find areas for improvement.

Realize that you are in a unique position to ask someone about processes they follow that might not already be documented. This is why you are creating flowcharts. You are drawing visual maps of the company itself and its inner workings.

One of the hardest things about the business practice is building repeatable processes that will guarantee or get you the closest outcome to what pushes the business forward. When you have a lot of people involved, especially if you have a lot of people who have been there for a long time, those processes start becoming part of people, and they transfer or translate very well.

Remember that a flowchart is something that you can show someone, with nodes and links. It is something that you can use in presentations. You can follow the flow of data, tracking it from person to person. It is proof of work that has been completed and showcases work that still needs to be done. It is a place to expand ideas. This is where people will return when they get lost, and it is a place where they might find their own ideas. It must be clear and concise, and must communicate your exact message to be the best possible tool for everyone who has a copy.

Flowcharts and documentation also serve as gateways to new ideas and to more people opening up to you. Let's say you've created a flowchart on the sales funnel. A copy finds its way to the head of sales, who says to you, "You've got part of this wrong. We don't go to market this way at all." You've opened up a conversation to find out what the head of sales is seeing and how to get to the bottom of the problem. You've started a conversation using a tool you built.

To illustrate how flowcharting can help you, here's a story:

I was once the new CTO of a company where I inherited a contract with a large enterprise customer. Suffice it to say that no one really knew what my predecessor had built, and the documentation was nonexistent. We were also a relatively small player inside of a larger ecosystem, so it was easy to get lost in who was obligated to deliver what to whom.

To make matters worse, it was in the government sector, and up until that point, I hadn't had much experience in that domain. The contract was up for renewal, and relationships were in disarray due to turnover of personnel.

Here's how I handled it:

1. I started setting up calls upstream so that I could introduce myself as the new CTO. This also gave me an opportunity to ask all the "dumb" questions I could about the project. I recorded these calls where possible so that I could replay and learn.

2. I regularly went back to my C-suite to not only give them updates on what I found, but also to have them educate me on various terms and conventions used in the industry. I will admit that this was hard. Not so much because I had to ask the questions the first time, but because I felt like I had to ask the same questions over and over so that I could eventually get comfortable with the overall ecosystem.

3. I opened a graphing tool (I really like OmniGraffle), and with every meeting I had, I would make sure to update that graph.

4. With each update to the graph, I went back to key players in the organization to run the graph by them so that they could see that I was learning and to give them the opportunity to correct me.

What I ended up with is included here for your reference.

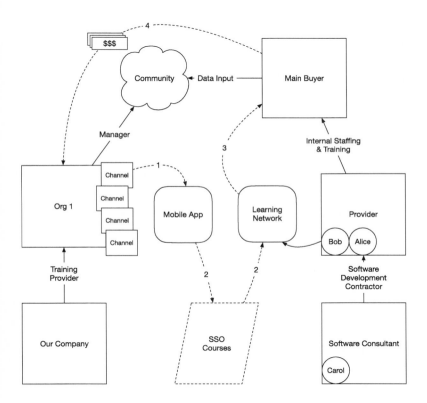

Presenting this graph to my C-suite and key players inside our company bought me a ton of goodwill because, for many of them, it was the first time they had seen these relationships on paper.

INTRODUCING YOUR STRATEGY

It's time to introduce your strategy to the company. You've delivered a sense of value with your quick win, and you've learned a lot about the company. You have an outsider's view of many of the issues, and you have solutions. The rest of the team has been asking about the next step and is excited to learn how you plan to proceed.

At this point, the team has good feelings toward you because you've worked to put them there. There is a feeling of "Wow, this person was able to come in, understand our business, make suggestions, and implement an idea that helped us out last month. I wonder how they will help us next?"

You want to evangelize that strategy. What is it? What will you accomplish with this company? Even if you don't yet have a solid strategy, you are ready to present ideas because you've been researching the company. You are ready to show the C-suite how your involvement with the company will be beneficial over the next twelve months, for example. You will present your long-term strategy.

Since you have some leverage because you have won some goodwill through your quick win, you now have to work on taking on a potentially complex system of revenues, products or services, pricing plans, churn, customer profiles, and all of the different ways this business makes money. How are you, as CTO, going to use technology to put this company on a strategy that fulfills its financial goals?

Think of your strategy as an iceberg. Above the water, you'll have a piece that is tangible, is visible—it's that *wow* factor. But there is potentially a lot of work that must be done beneath that water line, beneath the surface, which could include things like fixing broken processes, optimizing the performance, or getting rid of technical debt.

But as the CTO, what is your role right now? If you have VPs of engineering and product, these are the types of discussions that you're having with them. If you don't have them, you're working with your engineering leads to figure out what's holding you back, what moves you forward, where are your deficiencies? And you want to get to a place where you can communicate to your C-suite that this is your one, two, three plan for the organization.

These are the basics, but what I think is important for the CTO here is communication and packaging of that strategy. I think it's a great idea to name your plan. Speak to your C-suite in the form of named plans. I like the idea of saying this is the "Eighth Player" plan or this is the "Data Ownership" plan, or helping your company and your C-suite understand the plan better through the name, such as the "Revenue Expansion" plan.

If you introduce it as something named, then it's going to be a lot easier for you to bring people into that context when you're explaining it later. The thing about plans and the thing about visions and strategies is that they must be overcommunicated.

On a weekly basis, if not a daily basis, your plan will be challenged. The one challenge with a named plan, from my experience, is that your team may attach a meaning to the plan that veers from the original intent.

So if you talk about the "Hybrid Teams" plan as a way for engineers to work from anywhere they want, it could gradually turn into a plan where engineers have to work from certain locations around the world. So every time you say "Hybrid Teams" plan, you interpret it one way and others may interpret it another. You're talking about the "same plan," but really, you're not.

Your plan will also be challenged. It will be challenged by either people who don't believe in it, people who don't understand it, or circumstances that present themselves that you did not expect. I think it's incredibly important in month two to have a named plan or a named strategy. It doesn't have to be just one, but it's going to be something that you keep bringing back to the leadership team to reiterate how to push the ball forward on that plan. Just understand and expect that your plan will be challenged along the way.

I mentioned earlier in the book that I joined an organization that had a few large enterprise clients that had fallen into disarray due to employee churn. In my second month as CTO, I created the "Contracts Strategy." The strategy was designed to audit all contracts, understand the scope of work, build relationships with vendors and customers, and get us back on track for renewals. It was easy for the organization to understand what I was working on because all I had to say was that my actions were part of the "Contracts Strategy" and everyone understood the importance.

After you've formulated your plan, you must present it to the team. The way I would recommend is that you break it down into a drawing or a figure. You want to anchor people's brains to what you're trying to do. You want people to adopt an attitude of understanding the business mechanism that the technology will support. Gather the information into pie charts and bar graphs to make presenting it really easy.

I remember working at a company where we had an audacious plan to move from one-time revenue to a subscription model. The team, mostly millennials, was afraid of this plan. They kept pushing back on the plan for two reasons: One, it meant that they had to move to a product delivery that was new to them, so it involved learning new things. Two, they were scared that the only way they knew how to make money was being replaced by the only way they didn't know how to make money and that they would all lose their jobs.

I found myself having to repeat the "Mini Courses" plan over and over again, and eventually I adopted a hand gesture that made it really easy for me to remind everyone about the plan every day. I literally held up my left hand and slowly lowered it while slowly raising my right hand. This demonstrated how the plan was going to get rid of the old revenue and replace it with the new but that it was going to be a gradual process. The keyword was *gradual*, and that seemed to allay everyone's fears. After two years, we succeeded in that plan.

A FRAMEWORK FOR PRESENTATIONS

A useful way to create presentations is the Pelican Framework. *Pelican* is an acronym for creating perfect presentations and blog posts. It includes seven stepping stones that help you create something that clearly communicates the message you want to send. The acronym stands for:

Problem. The problem statement is the hook. There is no doubt that if you do not clearly articulate what problem you solved or are solving, people simply won't care. This is an essential way to make sure the right people are receiving the information.

Expertise. You've got their attention. Show them why they should care. This is where you insert the company goals and show them how your strategy aligns.

Learning. Describe solutions to problems you've uncovered. This is where we begin getting into the good stuff. This is where the C-suite will sit up and take notice because these are the answers they've been seeking.

Iterate. This is where you show your C-suite the easy-to-follow steps to iterate where they are today and where they will be after your strategy is implemented.

Contrarian. At this stage, someone might object to your framework. Spend time addressing these concerns and help him or her accept the overall package. Alternatively, find solutions together that include his or her ideas to help foster acceptance.

Again. Repeat yourself. Summarize your ideas in short bursts of tangible information.

Next steps. Now what? What will you do when you walk out of this meeting? What do you expect from others to help you reach the goals you just revealed? Go over next steps to help your strategy move forward.

Learn more about the Pelican Framework in the appendix.

It's important to remember that this is the first meeting about your idea. You don't have to walk away from it with a clear set of answers. You might have three or four meetings to reveal your full proposal. You might have meetings with different departments at different times. You are working together as an ongoing team to solve issues and build a better company. Don't feel like you need all the answers up front.

Communication is key here, so make sure you break down your ideas and plans into bite-sized chunks and that you're using language that your team understands. I also find it super helpful to communicate back to the CEO what he or she has told you over the past few weeks during these meetings to solidify that you are truly hearing him or her.

You prove that you are listening and that you care about this company's vision. Depending on the past experiences of the team, you may need to regain trust in the technology implementation. Showing them that you hear them is a great way to build up and maintain this trust.

When it comes to working with teams, it would behoove us to remember that even the simplest of plans can become a miscommunication nightmare. This is why your presentation must be written out in visual form and why you need to present it in a way that is consumable by everyone. It helps to have copies of the presentation to hand out, too, giving your audience a tangible place to take notes and to refer to later.

The mind of the CTO is full of knowledge because it has to be. You have to know everything about the company to create the best possible solutions. When it comes to working with teams, remember that each team member is focused on his or her specific issue. People may not be able to see the big picture the way you can, so breaking down the presentation into consumable chunks geared toward the audience provides better results.

What you're doing with this presentation is recognizing that there is a huge flow of information and that a blueprint for moving forward is necessary. You create something that people can refer back to and speak to as your plan unfolds over the next few weeks or months. You need to take that next step and write out all the possible implications of what you're saying and do the hard work of determining how that affects different departments. Everyone needs to know what to expect and how to go about doing the thinking and the homework.

Another way to look at this big reveal is to consider it a working document. It is more than an idea, or a meeting, or a Power-Point presentation. It is a document that you have to open up and write on. You are opening up not only your plan, but the people who need to help the plan succeed. You're demonstrating that you have thought about this, you've done the research, you've thought through the implications, and you care enough about the organization as a whole to do all that.

Clearly, you're going to synthesize some ideas with maybe a statement or a question. Sometimes, when I communicate a strategy, I like to tell people, "I have a plan. I have some ideas. I'm thinking through all the concepts, and here's what I think."

I want to demonstrate to the CEO that I am thoughtful, and I think in a C-suite where you have to have hundred-mile-a-minute-style conversations and ideas, you want to demonstrate thoughtfulness and a retrospective or even an introspective disposition. You want to deliver the message in a way that makes the CEO think, *Wow, he didn't just make this up on the spot; this was thoughtful. This was well thought out.*

The CEO trusts you to know the right route. He or she spent time getting to know you during your volunteer work and your interview phase. Even if he or she doesn't fully understand the technology, you do. You are being trusted to create something the CEO doesn't fully understand. So specifically for those CEOs, I made very sure that I named the plan, that the plan had a visual that they could remember and understand, and that there was a place for him or her to come back to later.

GETTING FEEDBACK

This is one of the most difficult topics because you're opening yourself up for disappointment. We want to feel valued, and we want to be validated for our work. Sometimes it's just easier for me to ignore potential missed expectations and replace those with some rationale for moving forward. But we must sometimes face the music.

As opposed to assuming that someone in your C-suite will speak up if they have feedback for you, a.k.a. no news is good news, find some time on their calendar and ask them the following questions:

- What's working for you in our relationship?

- What areas do you feel could use some tweaking?

- Is there anything you'd like me to do differently?

You're asking if your progress is satisfactory and if there is anything you can do to improve upon your existing performance. It's always easier if you seek the feedback before having it offered to you. Internally, though, it is sometimes tough to hear if the feedback isn't what you expected. Use the grounding method mentioned before (dig your heels into the floor), remember to breathe, and follow these tips to accept good or bad feedback with grace and dignity:

Recognize good intentions. Whether you've asked for the feedback or not, recognize that the person providing it isn't trying to hurt your feelings. They are offering a unique critique on your work to help you improve overall. Every piece of feedback will make you stronger if you put aside your feelings and consider how it will best serve you in your role. Also, if you asked for the feedback, you own the frame for this conversation. It's your conversation. You get to control it.

Actively listen. Stay engaged with the conversation. When someone says, "I like what you did here, but..." don't zone out after that *but*. We tend to check out at this point because we start obsessing over what we did wrong to bring it about. Instead, listen to what comes after it. "I like what you did here, but the CFO ran the numbers, and we just don't think it's in the budget." Oh. You missed something in the budget that affects your plan. *Okay*, you think, *I have to look for budgetary issues.* You've heard the feedback, and you know where to go next.

Ask questions. You don't need to take feedback at face value. You are allowed to ask questions. "Oh," you respond, "I didn't realize that wasn't in the budget. Do you think there's a disconnect between sales and finance somewhere?" You're letting the other person know a few things:

- You heard them, and you recognized their expertise.

- You acknowledge the issue.

- You are ready to collaborate on solutions.

Asking questions after receiving feedback is part of that natural curiosity you need to be the best. A solution isn't always imminent, but what always remains is the curiosity that helps you find the path toward possible solutions. With a curiosity mindset, you demonstrate a willingness to hear the person out and accept their feedback with an open mind.

When you realize the true value of feedback and use it to your advantage, your job becomes easier. Remember that every company is different. Each will have its own separate needs. You are still learning in month two; feedback will tell you if you're getting it right. If you're not, it's still okay—you still have that plausible deniability. Use it for now, but remember to also use the feedback to improve your performance because that deniability will eventually go away.

Responding to feedback positively also helps you become more approachable to the team. Giving feedback is just as hard as receiving it. Few people want to make someone feel bad. When you respond positively and work proactively together to address the feedback, they recognize you as someone who cares about the business.

Over time, people become less nervous about offering feedback because they feel safe with you. You create a gateway to finding more problems, and therefore more solutions, for the company overall when you keep yourself open and respond well to feedback.

Flowcharts are a tremendous tool that we technical people have to describe the current state of affairs to nontechnical people. They are also an indispensable tool for drawing out your strategy for the future state. Who doesn't like drawings? The fun lies in simplifying our drawings over time so that even the most complex ideas can be communicated to our executive teams.

Drawing flowcharts may make you feel like you're getting your hands dirty. But wait until you see just how dirty our hands are about to get.

CTO JOURNAL EXERCISES: DAYS 51—60

1. What is your technology strategy for this company?

2. What do you anticipate will be the hardest part of this strategy for the C-suite to swallow?

3. Describe some ideas for what you can flowchart this week:

    a. Who is the intended audience?

   b. What problem are you solving?

   c. How does the solution impact the team?

4. Describe the feedback session you had with a fellow C-suite team member:

   Name:

   a. What is working well for them in your relationship?

   b. What aspects of your relationship need tweaking?

   c. What can you do to further improve your relationship?

12

DAYS 61–70: LEARN TO IMPROVISE

THE NEED TO IMPROVISE COMES FROM THE FACT THAT anything can, and will, go wrong in business. Sometimes, when things go wrong, they do so quickly and without warning. This is when you will improvise. This is more than putting out fires on a daily basis; this is acting in a manner that will handle every company surprise, no matter the size or time frame.

The fact is that improvisation in anything takes practice. What do you do when something goes wrong? How do you react when a sudden change disrupts the whole routine? How do you turn it around to create something beneficial? You need to be able to think on your feet and act quickly in some situations. You need to become a skilled improviser.

Improvisation is a key factor in organizational agility, and it relies on a cool, calm head. This is how you will steer the company through crises and paradigm shifts involving both internal and external changes. You can certainly bet there was plenty of improvisation happening when COVID-19 hit, and the companies that did it best came out most successful. Developing these skills is no piece of cake, though. It takes years of practice, but don't panic. If you haven't learned good improv yet, you can still pick it up right now. Let's go over the three basic types of improvisation:

Imitative. This is the beginning of improv, and you probably do this already. It consists of observing what others are doing and matching their responses. For example, if your main trade company suddenly goes belly up, and everyone around you is scrambling to research their competitors, you might be inclined to do that too. After all, you want to solve the problem right away, right? It's a nice start to reacting to a crisis, but there are better ways to handle it.

Reactive. This type of improv factors in both the environment and other people to develop a reaction. You are not looking to others to react; you are looking at the pulse of the crisis. In this scenario, you might be researching competitors, but you're also considering the product and how it is transported. Is it transported via truck? Are your coworkers scrambling to find a new trucking company? Have they considered trains? You're looking at the environment as well as the other players in your reaction.

Generative. This is the highest level of improvisation and the easiest to forget if you're in crisis mode. This is when you try to anticipate what might happen in the future rather than responding to what's already happened. It is the riskiest because it is speculative—who could have known that your best form of transport was going to go bankrupt last night? But when you use generative improv, you've already built a list of not only other trucking companies, but railways and other forms of transport for your product. You have them organized by price and convenience for your company. You were ready for a crisis even before you knew you had to be.

It's easy to see why you would want to get to the generative stage. However, recognize that different situations might require different levels to find the best solution. While it's rare that imitative improv works for businesses, there might be situations where it solves the problem. View each situation at face value to figure out which type of improv might help fix it.

So how do you develop these improv skills that seem so successful in helping you put out these fires? It begins with you. You need to assess if you are competitively or collaboratively oriented. Chances are, as a CTO, you are collaboratively oriented, so let's begin by understanding your competitive counterparts.

Competitive people develop reactive improv faster because they act on all the information given to them from all sources. In the example above, the reactive improvisation personality is scrambling to find a new trucking company and competing with coworkers to find one as fast as possible. This is fine for the short term but could alienate your coworkers over time.

Let's say you react this way every time. Are you giving someone else a chance to shine? Remember, you're here to be a cheerleader. How are you supporting the team if you're not giving anyone else a chance to strut their stuff?

Collaborative individuals, however, take longer to develop reactive improv skills because they hesitate to seize every opportunity for themselves. They prefer to watch how others react, how the environment reacts, and how their previous preparation might help the situation.

When a huge emphasis is placed on collaboration, it can shut down initial growth, and perhaps a large group of customers misses out because the product wasn't put onto the first possible truck right away. In the end, however, you and your coworkers gain social connectedness and insight into how to solve future problems.

Now that you know the basics of improvisation, how do you apply it to your overall workday?

Build an awareness of how these skills develop around you. Understand how both a competitive and a collaborative mindset affect the business. Learn to identify teams or individuals who already possess terrific improvisation skills, assigning them to open-ended or unstructured projects.

Find that balance. Collaboration and competition both seem to have negative and positive traits. It's time for you to find that balance. Find ways to help collaborative employees incorporate some competitiveness, and vice versa. Growth over time requires both types of personalities in improvisation, so eliminating either is a recipe for disaster.

Don't forget to keep building social structures. Fostering true generative skills requires a psychologically safe place with social interactions that build trust for collaboration. Employees learn to gain inspiration from each other's nuances, working together to find new ideas without fear of rejection. While this environment is sometimes hard to maintain, it will benefit the company long term.

Again, remember that this requires a cool, clear head. If you tend to react negatively to bad situations initially by getting mad or flying off the handle, reassess yourself. Figure out why, and work to change this. When the whole building is on fire, the rest of the team might look to you as the leader who can fix it all. Hold on to your head, ground yourself, and be the person who can bring everyone back to Earth. Be the person who can improvise and make any situation work for the company.

GET YOUR HANDS DIRTY

You should be doing this already, but if you're not, it's time to start. You've gotten to know the company and you've built a plan for moving forward; now it's time to get in the trenches with your team.

Nothing is worse than a technical leader who shows reluctance in helping people, no matter how small or seemingly insignificant the issue. As the CTO, if someone comes to you because the printer isn't showing up on the local network anymore, you need to go troubleshoot the problem. I believe that you demonstrate your leadership by doing the jobs that seem small to you.

You are the only technical person in the room. Yes, you are going to try to get the PowerPoint to show up on the screen. Yes, you're going to try to fiddle with the Apple TV. Yes, you're going to try to figure out why the Wi-Fi isn't working. That stuff not only keeps you humble, but it also keeps you in good standing with the team. You are showing them that you are there for them, that you are approachable, and again, that you care about them getting their work done and being successful.

Nontechnical people often lump all technology under the umbrella of what you should be doing. Sure, you know you've got much bigger fish to fry, but keeping up the goodwill by working in the dirty trenches of rebooting a router on occasion helps your team trust you when you really need it later.

Another great way to get your hands dirty and to show your team you support them is to organize a group event. Now that you've spent some one-on-one time with key members of your team, even if your team consists of only you and one other person, I recommend focusing on some sort of event.

This could be as "boring" as a lunch or something a little more exciting like go-kart racing or pier fishing. The idea here is to demonstrate your leadership skills. You just rolled out an extensive plan for the company; help them believe you can make it happen by showcasing leadership capabilities. If you're going to lead the charge in building up the product, you should show leadership in the little things. Demonstrate that you can put together a fun event for your team. There are so many nuances in planning a group event that somebody could write a book on just that topic alone.

I would suggest that the activity include something to do plus something to eat. Dinner and a movie? Oh yes. While everyone else is having fun, you're working. You're making mental notes about interactions, excitement, and reluctance. You're watching for changes in interactions since you've been there, and you're silently assessing yourself. Have you helped improve interactions within the company?

I suggest the following logistics for your outing:

- Have a designated videographer or photographer.

- Avoid alcohol.

- Pick a time and place and make sure you give everyone a heads-up at least a month in advance.

- Don't change the date, even if people can't make it.

- If you have a remote team and the budget, try to help them meet in a central location. Fly them if necessary.

Of course, you'll have your CTO journal.

CTO EMAIL ROUTINE AND UPDATE

During this month, it's also wise to establish a monthly CTO email routine. You're updating the executive team by communicating some key points. I recommend keeping it to three bullet points. For example:

> Subject: Monthly CTO Update for June 2019
>
> Hi team,
>
> It's been an awesome couple weeks at ACME, and I thought I'd shoot out a quick update for your information:

- The executive sync-up last week was incredibly helpful, so thank you for taking the extra time to walk me through the customer success process.

- I really enjoyed the product brainstorm session we had. Things got pretty heated, but I loved the collaboration. I am planning some more flowchart sessions for this month.

- We had an epic developmental evening. Please find full details in a follow-up email.

Please ping me with any questions you may have.

Alice

This is where your journal comes in handy, since your thoughts and actions are all documented there. Your team has tangible evidence of your work, and you have a paper trail of communication. It's a win for everyone.

When we started this chapter, you thought that getting your hands dirty meant coding, didn't you? I'm so sorry, not sorry to disappoint you. But doesn't it feel great to have helped and served your team in the smallest of ways? How did the outing with your engineering team go?

We will now turn our attention to the C-suite because we are entering the zone where we may have missed some commitments. We may also be fielding questions from the executive team that we didn't expect.

CTO JOURNAL EXERCISES: DAYS 61–70

1. What group activity did you take your team to?

2. What were some of the standout moments?

Use this for future outings when you need to reconnect your team or just take a break from company business.

1. List five to ten IT and technology tasks that you feel are beneath you in this company.

2. Which one will you execute in the next few days?

•

13

DAYS 71–80: MAINTAIN TRUSTING RELATIONSHIPS

You just arrived at the three-quarter mark of the 100-day journey to CTO Excellence! By now you are a force to be reckoned with in the company. Hopefully your voice is heard and your presence sought out in the company. Ever hear the saying "the tallest trees catch the most wind"? Well, during the final weeks of your journey, you'll most likely catch some wind. Don't fret; we're in this together!

You've worked hard to build relationships with your team. They know you can do the job through your quick win, and they're excited for your overall strategy. In month three, continue working on these relationships to maintain that high trust level. This is a game of trust, not a game of issues or issue resolution. Yes, there are necessary resolutions, but they will never be realized without a maintenance of trust.

Stay focused on what the team is committed to and what you, as a group, are delivering on. What are you establishing, for your team and for your C-suite, how the next few years look with you as the leader?

Technology becomes this black hole to someone who doesn't understand it. They think it can fix many problems, but it really doesn't fix everything. Again, it's not the magic that comes out of your nonexistent magic wand.

Learn to look for how people can get to solutions without technology to help maintain their trust in you. When you lean on their strengths to solve problems and show them that their specific expertise will work next to the technology, they keep that good feeling they've had all along about you. They trust that you continue to see all aspects of the problem.

Remember, as well, to pay attention to even the smallest details that you've communicated to your team. We might get into the habit of taking on small projects, or saying, "Yes, I'll look into that," just to have something to say. Be careful with that. What seems like a small task to you, and maybe meaningless, will be a big deal to the person needing it done. More important than the task is the broken promise.

Let's say there's a broken monitor in a conference room. There are other places to hold presentations, but Sam likes that conference room best. He's asked you to look into the issue, and you said you would. It seems like a small thing to you, especially now that you're working on your strategy. However, you said you'd do it, and if you don't, you'll have to start from square one with Sam.

Remember, too, to give those around you insight into your process. They can't read your mind. For example, perhaps you were sending weekly updates to your CEO, but she didn't respond. You might think, *Well, those updates must not be that important.* Don't assume. Those updates might be why she doesn't feel the need to come ask how you're doing, and it might be part of her ongoing trust in you. The weekly email suggested above should continue into this month and beyond, just to maintain that sense of trust you worked so hard to gain.

Trust is the most fragile thing you will handle in your role. It breaks with a breath. Be careful to maintain it once you have it.

WHEN THE EXECUTIVE TEAM STARTS VEERING FROM YOUR STRATEGY

This will happen for a number of reasons. Never forget the humanness of the company. People might forget about your plan, get caught up in something else, or try to implement their own "fixes" to your overall idea.

It's hard not to get defensive when your carefully crafted tech or product strategy is questioned or forgotten. It's harder when the team all agreed to it just a few weeks ago. This is natural. This is an opportunity to iterate. The beauty of iterating is that you get to incorporate what you learn from others into your future decisions.

Indeed, that is what makes decision-making so valuable: the ability to learn. The executive team will learn, and they will come to their own conclusions. Sometimes this will look like they've lost faith in your proposed strategy. Their ignorance or lack of support might make you feel exposed and draw out your offensive strategy. This could look like calling for meetings out of frustration to reiterate your plan or making unilateral decisions that affect other departments without any notice.

I think there is a better way to approach this than to go on the offensive. You can make the executive team feel heard without emboldening them around a completely different plan. This isn't so much about right or wrong as it is about the ability to rally the executives around you and to trust that if you can't rally them, then your plan needs a rethink.

Start off by saying that you're not married to a plan over and above the shared success of the company that everyone in the room is pursuing. State that, for the purposes of this meeting, you'd like to put the current plan on the whiteboard as an option, but that you're open to discussing variations of the plan as plans B, C, or D. Go to the whiteboard, draw a few columns, and write your current plan in the first column.

Step 1. Listen to their take on your current plan by asking powerful questions. Dive deeper into what they're saying. Ask questions to get more answers and to get behind their ideas. You may be faced with "I don't understand how this plan..." or "Remind me again why..." or the dreaded, "My buddy has a company, and they..."

Step 2. Demonstrate that you're open to new directions and ideas by asking questions like "How would you go about..." or

"Given those thoughts, what do you think we should consider?" Don't see this as a negative or as a sign of weakness that you're not sticking to your original convictions. View this as intelligent, knowledgeable people coming to you with an alternative solution that just might work. If you've made yourself approachable over the past three months, this shouldn't be a tough step. If you can group the new ideas into a new plan, then go to the whiteboard, give the new plan a heading, and write down the main points of the plan in that column.

If all goes well, you will have a few plans, each in its own column. Please note that during this whole process you are the CTO, the leader facilitating various ways to execute the shared objective. You are not capitulating or checking out. You are active and engaged.

Step 3. Extract the concepts that are similar to the current strategy. This will go a long way to make them feel like they're being heard while you are organizing your thoughts. This could look like drawing circles around the similar concepts on the whiteboard or putting asterisks against the points that are the same. It's important to note that you are talking to nontechnical people, and they may have characterized technical steps differently, while you know that they are the same (in some cases).

Step 4. Do not use the phrases "We're saying the same thing," "This is what I said earlier in the conversation," or "I've been saying this all along." You're not trying to merge thoughts or conflate ideas. This could come across as self-serving and you being defensive about your plan. Instead, celebrate that there is diversity of thought and expression, and gently point to the circles and asterisks as points of commonality.

Step 5. Use a mixture of your concepts and theirs to build a new plan, and write down the steps in their own column. This could look very similar to your original plan, but it demonstrates that you're not married to being right. It shows that you are joined with them in both wanting the same outcome. Something more magical happens at this point, though: shared ownership. Your executive team feels like they, too, own the plan.

Step 6. With all the plans on the whiteboard, take a step back and have the team enjoy open discussion on those. As the CTO, review each plan with the same tone of voice in order not to show any bias. Of course, you can have your favorite plan and voice that, but don't use more words and enthusiasm for the plan you love and less on the others.

Step 7. Find agreement on which plan to proceed with. This will be easier if the plan remains somewhat similar to your original plan. It gets harder when there is an increase in cost due to work lost or time spent. But make sure you talk about this and help the executive team understand the implication.

Step 8. Commit to a quick follow-up meeting on this plan within two weeks. This gives everyone permission to see if their assumptions play out the way they thought. You are also committing as CTO to do the work necessary so that you'll have all the data necessary to show the team whether this new plan is on track or not.

We don't want our developers married to their coding language, our managers married to underperforming engineers, or our product people advocating for unvetted features. In the same way, we don't want our CTOs pushing for strategies without consideration for the executive team.

HANDLING MISSED COMMITMENTS

We've discussed this briefly, but it deserves its own section. By now, you've talked to a lot of people, you've said a lot of things, and you may have made promises that you never delivered on. What's going to end up happening is that, out of nowhere, someone will say to you, "Well, you said that you would do this," or "You said that it would be this way. It's not that way yet, so I'm concerned."

This has happened to me. I was in a meeting where I said to the founders, "We need to have values. We're going to work on our own set of values for the engineering team. We should really be able to have a set of values by which we hire and fire our engineers." I committed to getting that done. It wasn't something they asked for; it was something I suggested. It wasn't anything that was driving the business. It had zero perceived impact on the business—from their perspective, it was just frosting on the cake that would make the daily process a little sweeter.

What it did, though, was create an unfinished loop in the COO's head. After nearly a year went by, she approached me and brought it up. We were in a contentious conversation about a completely different topic when she said, "Yeah, and by the way, I never saw those engineering values." I had no leg to stand on.

Simple comcepts may unravel because people don't understand what you're talking about. You know it's simple, it has minimal impact, and that it's a benign issue. But in that COO's head, values and vision and mission are valued above all else. These are core to running a people business, so the COO thinks, *The CTO still hasn't delivered that.* Now you have a running list of accusations or indictments with a case being built up against you.

It's basically an on-the-spot situation, and the challenge is that we want to get defensive, especially if we internalize criticisms or failed deliveries. It changes how we show up to the C-suite.

Remember that just because you know where your priorities lie, that doesn't mean everyone else understands. The COO hadn't spoken up because she assumed I had prioritized the project and was working on it, when in fact, it fell to the wayside because other things had to happen first. As it turns out, she was looking forward to what I was going to come up with.

What do you do if this happens to you? There are a few tips I've found that work well for saving face.

Talk. If you know you're going to miss a commitment, let the other person know right away. This gives them time to plan accordingly. It also shows them that you respect their needs, even if you'll be late meeting them. Apologize if you've already missed the deadline or, like me, you forgot about the promise altogether.

Never get defensive. Own your mistake and move forward with phrases such as "Yes, I missed that, and I'm sorry. How can we work together to move forward on this issue? What solutions would you like to see?" You're not getting defensive, and you're not handing over your power. You're working with the other person to find a solution to the issue while owning it at the same time.

Provide alternatives. What can you do to make it up? If getting the actual project done isn't an option, what can you do instead to deliver? Remember that you may have delivered on every other promise you've ever made, but the person in front of you only remembers your slight because it made him or her feel bad. At our most basic level, we remember how we felt in a moment, and that carries a lot of weight.

Meet the commitment. Can you still fulfill the promise? There is value in meeting all or part of the commitment. Work with the other person to find the answer to this. How much of the commitment can be met to satisfy the other person? Involve the other person in the solution and in the work to rebuild the good faith you've lost.

Follow through. This is essential. Make sure you follow through and fulfill the promise. Include the other person on email updates. Discuss the project with them as it's happening. Deliver on what you say you'll deliver. Most people realize you are a human and you will make mistakes. How you handle those mistakes is how you will be measured in the months to come.

In the spirit of future credibility for tough decisions, make sure that you are presently taking care of the small decisions. Become blameless wherever you can. Make sure you are blameless in the little things so you can be better recognized for the big things.

Because we deliver, because we, as CTOs, are constantly delivering, there is this dilemma of what to do when expectations are missed. There is an involuntary response because, as humans, we don't want to upset someone else. As professionals, we don't want to have to either miss deadlines or have things change in a way where what we said before doesn't apply right now. However, it's important to remember that we are all humans dealing with other humans who are all as flawed as we are. A little communication and follow-through will go a very long way.

We took a minute to recognize that business is messy. We aren't fortune tellers, and we're not perfect communicators. We are emotional beings grafted onto dynamic teams with a desire to belong and a mission to achieve. Things go wrong. The question is, how do we handle ourselves when we are ashamed or embarrassed about missing the very targets we were supposed to hit? We found the answer in this chapter. We now need to find the answers to the age-old CTO question: How do I manage my time?

CTO JOURNAL EXERCISES: DAYS 71–80

1. List the concerns or objections your executive team has raised to you (this could be about other people as well).

2. Which commitments have you made that you either forgot about or simply did not deliver on?

14

DAYS 81–90: CREATE "WHAT IF" SCENARIOS

WHILE THE THIRD MONTH IS ALL ABOUT OPERATIONAL STABILITY, it is also a time to improvise and innovate. You're not quite at cruising altitude yet, but you're getting there. You're past plausible deniability, you've got a few wins, you have a plan in place, and you're looking toward the future. You'll start saying, "I can do this. I have a strategy for that. This is what I'm bringing to that issue." You're improvising and you're understanding. You're strategizing. Armed with two months of data, you start to gain a better picture of the current situation and the company, and you begin to create "what if" scenarios.

You should be running "what if" scenarios to create possibilities for your company. We know that many ideas die on the vine because of some obstacle that seems insurmountable at the time. Some examples of "what if" scenarios could include:

- What if we knew all our users' annual income? We'd be able to show higher donation amounts to higher-income users and lower donation amounts to lower-income users.

- What if we could release this feature within the next two weeks? We'd be able to leverage the upcoming conference as a way to see if users would be interested in the new direction we want to take our app.

- What if customer success had the necessary access to run the cancellation script? We'd be able to save many hours of developer time and distraction.

I'm not saying that obstacles are like a tiny dog barking at you and that you should shove them away with a flick of your foot. Obstacles are heavy and, in many cases, require a ton of effort to address, especially when they require a change for your customers. But—what if you could overcome those obstacles? What possibility exists beyond that? The role of CTO here is tricky because you have to overcome two obstacles yourself:

- Rid yourself of "realism" in which your own mind frets over the obstacles to innovative ideas. You would need to cultivate the "what if" mindset for yourself and develop an authentic belief in the realm of what is possible. If you don't have this belief, you won't be able to overcome the next point.

- Facilitate this belief in others so that they can embrace the "what if" mindset. This is where the rubber meets the road because you would be an advocate for new thinking while simultaneously taking on the burden of removing the obstacle that stands in the way of your colleagues' own faith that what is possible can actually be achieved.

The benefits to "what if" thinking include:

Better performance. Operational and financial performance are both improved using this method. Getting rid of the extra step, the unnecessary wait time, or the lag in approval time will optimize operations not only internally, but also for your customers. Removing wasteful steps can also have a great impact on team morale.

Quick turnaround. Decisions can be made faster when wasteful steps are removed and the right people are in the room. With a "what if" mindset, there is also more freedom to discuss ways to improve processes. Like a muscle getting its daily exercise, the process of adjusting, or going from possibility to reality, shortens, and the benefits are felt quicker.

Planning. This is a wonderful but also slightly tricky benefit to "what if" scenarios. Building it into your planning and design phase allows for addressing potential inefficiencies that may occur when the project is completed. This allows the team to prepare for this at the onset of the project. The trickiness comes in when these planning meetings spend too much time on phantom scenarios that may not occur at all. This could lead to overengineering. But yes, if this is done right, it leads to better planning.

ORGANIZE YOUR TIME

While you're improvising, teaching others to do so, and building a better society within the company, you're continuing to observe. By this month, you've observed a certain cadence in the company regarding meetings, socialization, and collaboration. This is a good time to decide how you are going to block out your own time.

Assuming that most companies live and die by their shared calendars, it is time for you to make a few notes on how to divide up your day. You will be wearing multiple hats and adopting the same "company first" attitude as everyone else. Taking time for yourself might be misinterpreted as waning loyalty or depleted energy.

I've been in this situation far too often and have learned that a reckless, reactionary approach not only kills productivity, but it also leads to dangerous decision-making. You can't just do things willy-nilly. If you're not implementing block time in the beginning of month three, you need to start considering it. How will you do it? Will you give yourself time to gather your thoughts and process ideas on your own in the morning, and then fill your afternoon with meetings? Will you have early meetings followed by a gym break for yourself? Learning how to work in chunks and block off time is a key component in being a successful CTO.

Pull out your CTO journal and start a new page:

Blocking Out Time

1. When do most meetings seem to happen in this company?

2. How punctual are the meeting attendees?

	MONDAY	TUESDAY	WEDNESDAY	THURSDAY	FRIDAY
8-10AM	MEETING	MEETING	MEETING	MEETING	MEETING
10AM-NOON	MEETING	MEETING	MEETING	MEETING	MEETING
NOON-2PM	PERSONAL	PERSONAL	PERSONAL	PERSONAL	PERSONAL
2-4PM	REVIEW	REVIEW	REVIEW	REVIEW	REVIEW
4-6PM	OPEN	OPEN	OPEN	OPEN	OPEN

The five-day workweek columns highlight the best time to have meetings according to the company's existing schedule, and you've scheduled personal time. The personal time doesn't always have to be about relaxation, though it would be awesome if you could get that in when you needed it. It can also be for the things you can't get to because you're always putting out fires. For instance, the budget request from your CEO, or the technology overview write-up, or whatever other tasks can only be done by you.

You don't have to share this chart with your coworkers either. It can be something to keep to yourself because there are times when it has to be flexible. Meetings spill over, people can't meet up outside of your personal time, or there's a fire to put out while you're supposed to be reviewing your work on your own. It's important to stick to this as much as possible, but remember that it can be adjusted as needed as your time with the company grows.

In this chapter we saw that introducing "what if" scenarios goes a long way to helping the company explore new ideas and outcomes. It also introduces a level of volatility to our planning that we have to be aware of. This is why we also took a look at how you organize your time. You may have had your own time blocks coming into the company, but now you need to adjust to the company schedule.

Let's shift our attention to the stakeholders inside the company. Whether we like it or not, knowing who has influence and who is most tied to outcomes at the company will help us focus our energy as CTOs.

CTO JOURNAL EXERCISES: DAYS 81—90Y

Open a new page in your CTO journal and prepare the following:

1. List ten inefficiencies that exist in the company's process, products, or services today.

2. Write down the consequences that occur as a result of each inefficiency.

3. What obstacles stand in the way of removing those inefficiencies?

4. What possibilities exist when those obstacles are removed?

5. Draw what your ideal week looks like.

Monday	Tuesday	Wednesday	Thursday	Friday
Lunch	Lunch	Lunch	Lunch	Lunch

15

DAYS 91–100: UNDERSTAND WHAT IS TRULY IMPORTANT TO STAKEHOLDERS

YOU'RE IN THE FINAL STRETCH! CONGRATULATIONS ON getting through the first 90 days. You only have 10 days to go to attain CTO Excellence. Being a chief technology officer of the company means you understand what is at stake for the company. These last few days are essential in your excellence endeavor because they embody the role of every officer: working *on* the company and not being trapped *inside* the company.

This is an area filled with assumptions and riddled with uninformed guesses. Make it your mission to never guess what is important to your stakeholders. Pursue complete understanding of what they want from the business or project so that you can understand how to obtain it for them. The assumption would be that their desires align with the business goals, but make sure by understanding what is truly important to them.

In *Trillion Dollar Coach*, a book about Bill Campbell, who coached the likes of Eric Schmidt, Larry Page, and Steve Jobs, the authors mention a hard rule that Bill had when it came to stakeholders directing the work of engineering teams: "Never come to them with the solution. Come to them with the problem you're trying to solve so that they can come up with the solutions."

In the same way, make sure that you are not on the receiving end of a stakeholder's interpretation of the problem they're trying to solve. Find out what is important to the stakeholder.

Get to know the stakeholders to build your understanding of their needs by following these tips:

- Know who they are. Include a page in your CTO journal with their names, positions, and other pertinent information.

- Identify their place within the organization.

- Determine what you need from them. This will help you build on what they might need from you.

- Engage with the stakeholders by inviting yourself to those meetings.

- Revisit the page in your CTO journal, filling in information and completing a flowchart similar to the one you built for the C-suite.

Use this information to build a team, just like you did when you were working on getting to know your C-suite. Many people find stakeholders intimidating. Remember, they are humans like the rest of us.

COACH STAKEHOLDERS AROUND INSIGHTS

How do you get stakeholders wrapped around your ideas? How do you coach them to appreciate your insights? You need a stakeholder engagement plan.

A stakeholder engagement plan identifies the actions required to encourage stakeholders to have productive involvement in your outlined strategy. You want to pull these people into your ideas and show them how they will be affected positively if they help you with your plan.

Using the stakeholder information from your CTO journal, start getting them talking to each other if they aren't already. Invite key stakeholders to project meetings to find and resolve conflicts as soon as possible.

While interacting with them, try to understand them before trying to get them to understand you. This puts you in a position of trust because you're listening to them. People like to feel like they're being heard. Don't forget all those great listening techniques you practiced when getting to know your team. In fact, pull them out in spades when interacting with stakeholders. Really, truly listen to each one.

Make sure you're leading with integrity and having meaningful engagements. Say what you mean, and mean what you say.

Do what you say you will do to show them they can trust you to handle any support you might get from them. Engage them in estimates and expected outcomes to help them understand what they're in for.

The stakeholders are a team, just like the team you're leading in the office. Treat them as such. Build trust and show confidence in your plan to encourage them to get on board with you.

Complete your stakeholder engagement plan following these five steps:

1. Classify them. Each stakeholder can be placed into a defined group. For example, they can be clumped into "supporting" or "opposed" to your proposed strategy.

2. Develop a power and interest grid. This is an analysis tool. It shows the power of any specific stakeholder on a y-axis and the interest level on an x-axis. This will give you a visual of the stakeholder's "stake" in your project.

3. Define each person's power. You need to know how much power each stakeholder has. Be careful here, though, because even the smallest stakeholder could change the project. You need to pay attention to all of them in some capacity.

4. Define interest. How interested are they all, really?

5. Develop your overall engagement plan. Prioritize each stakeholder by power and influence. Specify the frequency and type of communication according to this priority.

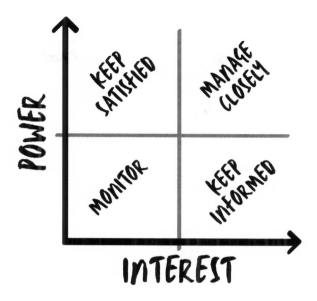

In this chapter we learned how to be shrewd in our relationships with powerful people. For most of us, this could feel like the most disingenuous way to show up. But we ignore this aspect of business at our own peril, especially in our own seat of power, called the seat of the chief technology officer.

CTO JOURNAL EXERCISES: DAYS 91–100

1. Review the following sample CTO journal page, helping you get to know each individual stakeholder:

Stakeholder Information

Name:

Title:

Power: Low or high?

Influence: Low or high?

Current level of engagement with company and/or project:

Desired level of engagement:

Interests:

Concerns:

1. Start a new page in your CTO journal for a stakeholder engagement plan:

Stakeholder Engagement Plan

Stakeholder list: Names of everyone

Project phase: Most likely, you're at the beginning.

Contact names: Do you call the stakeholder directly or communicate with an assistant?

Areas of influence: Basically, the stakeholders' "stake." This is where their interests influence the project.

Power: How much power does each stakeholder have to stop and/or change the project?

Engagement approach: How do you engage each stakeholder?

KNOWING THE ROPES AND MOVING FORWARD

16

WORK WITH OTHERS

IT'S TIME TO ACT ON YOUR STRATEGY! YOU'VE BUILT A FOUN-
dation. People like you, and they trust you. They know you'll
deliver when you say you will. You have the stakeholders on
board, and your tech team is ready to roll out your ideas. It's
time to reflect on what you've done and consider how you will
move forward.

Part 3 adds more tools to your quiver—tools that I have found
to be most useful in my tenure as a CTO at various companies.
We'll take a look at one of my most popular frameworks for
remaining calm and collaborative when your CEO throws new
ideas at you. It is called "Flying with Your CEO," and I have
a video on YouTube describing this in more detail. I've also
faced many interrogations in the C-suite that I know you have
faced, or will soon. My hope is that you'll find yourself coming
back to this part of the book as you face these challenges so
that you can be the world-class leader that your company
deserves.

A NOTE ABOUT MEETINGS AND LEARNING TO FLY WITH YOUR CEO

At times, you'll encounter a CEO who has technical chops and strong opinions on how the technology should be used. The easy way out of dealing with these personalities is to say, "Tell me what to do, and I'll get it done." That's great for the short term, but it damages long-term trust. It also is not the habit of a great CTO. Instead, consider using the Flying with Your CEO Framework.

Ideation conversations are an opportunity. They are meetings that can cement your leadership and facilitation skills. But they are tough. We are tempted to capitulate. But bare-knuckle these conversations!

You have the ability to bring the best out of your CEO. You are the person who will help him or her fly while staying grounded in reality. During these meetings that you attend or set up yourself, you have an opportunity to guide the CEO in a direction that works best for the company overall.

Sometimes, ideas need to be sanity-checked and brought back to reality. Yes, a good idea has been presented, but maybe other steps need to be taken before implementing the idea. Maybe the idea is great but there are obstacles that need to be moved first. It is up to you to rein in the brainstorming when it wants to jump off the cliff without looking. Think of the process as a plane on a runway:

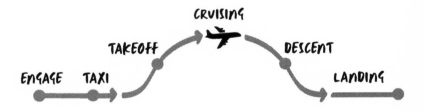

1. **Engage.** This is the moment when you get sucked into an ideation conversation that might feel ill-timed or unnecessary. Usually this is when you feel like priorities have already been set and are now being challenged by new ideas that may not have been vetted. Take a chair, sit at the whiteboard, take a deep breath, and engage! This looks like having a positive affect and a tone of optimism when you get asked to participate.

2. **Taxi.** As the conversation begins, you're doing all the listening to gain as much context as you can. Feel free to ask questions, take notes, and make sure you're getting the clear picture of why this is so important to the CEO or person communicating the idea. This is not an interrogation. This looks like being curious about where or how the idea originated.

3. **Take off.** This is where the conversation might get a bit noisy, shake you around a little bit, and cause an emotional response in you. Hold on to your seat, lean against your seat belt, and don't say a word! Just listen. The best thing to do here is to take notes.

4. **Cruise.** This is the reflection stage. You spend most of your time saying back to the person what you're hearing. The best-case scenario is that you're both standing around a whiteboard or some visual aid to communicate back to each other in a neutral medium versus talking at each other. The best outcome here is that you've processed what it will take to implement the idea or where it fits in the list of priorities.

5. **Descend.** Once you've given the conversation enough time to cruise, and you have an idea of where to go with it, strap on your seat belt again. This is where you start communicating the implications of moving forward with the idea. You're looking for head nods from the other person, but also expect some turbulence as you descend.

6. **Land.** This is where there needs to be a clear understanding of what you're each walking away with. Leave no word unspoken. If necessary, explicitly ask for next steps, but not as someone who has to go implement them. Ask as a partner discussing an idea.

TAXI	TAKE OFF	CRUISE	DESCEND	LAND
What to Do	**What to Do**	**What to Do**	**What to Do**	**What to Do**
Indicate that you are willing to engage in the conversation Prepare for steep takeoff	Listen actively Draw more ideas out from your CEO Ask more questions	Whiteboard ideas with your CEO Ask slightly deeper questions as a means to gain clarity or gently poke holes in their thinking Potentially start drawing nodes and links	Demonstrate a commitment and critically evaluate the idea Talk about priority and ask your CEO who they think would be great to work on this Help CEO understand what you're already working on Ask about how this impacts other functions within the company, e.g., marketing	Look at exiting the meeting, but without having made any commitments Indicate that you are willing to collaborate more on the idea
What Not to Do	**What Not to Do**	**What Not to Do**	**What Not to Do**	**What Not to Do**
Defer ownership Look for short-term solution to end conversation Ideate	Mentally check out of the conversation Try and do the implementation as they're speaking Assess cost or priority	Shoot down ideas Voice concerns	Engage in defensive posture Get upset Show feelings of disrespect or devaluing	Take responsibility and ownership to deliver just so you can exit the meeting Leave the conversation at an ambiguous point

TAXI	TAKE OFF	CRUISE	DESCEND	LAND
Example Phrases to Start the Conversation	Example Phrases to Move the Conversation	Examples of Yes/ No Technique	Example Phrases	Example Phrases to Leave without a Decision but Also without Being Ambiguous
"Sounds great; tell me about it." "I'd love to know more." "Interesting. Let's talk about it."	"So when you say X, are you saying that people would be able to do Y?" "Yes, and then…" "What sparked your enthusiasm about this?"	"What I hear you saying is…" "Is _____ a potential concern for you?" "Doe this feel the same as a previous scenario? (describe a scenario)"	"I am not totally convinced yet, but I can see where this could be a good approach." "Where does this fit in terms of company priorities?" "What type of time frames would be needed to make this successful?" "Are there other groups who might have input?"	"I'd love to talk about this some more. Can we set up a dedicated time to review?" "I'd like to get some input from (peers, teams, etc.)." "Let me do some research and follow up with you by (date)."

It's important to learn how to fly with your CEO to help the company and to help you keep doing what you need to do.

WHEN THEY COME AT YOU WITH TOOLS

There are times when the C-suite does something that requires you to have a cool head and a solid hold on your communication efforts. One Friday afternoon, I had a run-in with a VP. He came at me with a must-have tool that he felt he needed to use in order for him to do his job. It wasn't one of those isolated tools that he could use by himself but rather a CRM tool that he felt was essential for him to be able to do his job. It was a tool that no one else was using, would affect some business processes, and would require technical integration into our existing tool chain. No worries, he said. We could just use Zapier to integrate everything.

The request didn't reach me directly, as in, he didn't think of using the tool and then follow that up immediately with setting up a meeting to talk to the CTO about this. No, I got a phone call from him only when he was stumped by a Zapier error message while trying to build the integration himself.

Wow. Where to begin?

One of the fundamental values a CTO provides to their company is providing tools so that everyone can do their jobs with as little technical friction as possible. While we can't perfectly control which tools people bring into the company other than company policies and training, this responsibility does make us somewhat possessive of the tool chain used to serve business purposes. So how do I provide this VP with a sense of autonomy and excitement while also pissing all over his ideas for integrating his suite of tools?

On this particular Friday afternoon, I was out of town, so I had to manage some of this via Slack and phone calls. I detected urgency and frustration in his voice, and so I had to fight the urge to either break my back to help him or pull rank and match his frustration with my own. There was a range of emotions that came up for me, and it was important that I recognize that it was okay to feel those emotions but absolutely not okay to take them out on him.

There are steps you can take to handle a situation like this, and they relate to the previous chart highlighting how to bring the CEO down from cruising altitude.

SLOW DOWN

First, you need to establish a sense of calm. When you detect a level of urgency, the goal shouldn't be to change minds or question behavior. The first goal is to slow things down so you can come to a place of collaboration. The best way to do this is to focus on reassuring the other person that you both want the same things and that you are there to support them in their successes.

CONSIDER OTHER SOLUTIONS

Consider that their solution has a rightful place in the compendium of possible ways to solve this challenge. It is very important that you get them to agree to this by asking for a yes or no. You could say, "Your solution is solid. Would you mind if we explore other options in the name of due diligence?" If the answer is no, then we may have a different problem here.

The goal is not necessarily to consider other tools, but rather to gather more data to understand what, exactly, the problem is that you are trying to solve. Considering other solutions also demonstrates that you're willing to be a worthy collaborator.

HUMBLE YOURSELF

Establish that you are open to being wrong about the whole thing and that you look forward to implementing their solution if it turns out to be the best one. Remember that you have a strong leg to stand on when you declare that you may not have all the information or context they have. It will make them feel good about themselves, and hopefully they'll have some sympathy for you.

I have a problem with the phrase "I am willing to be wrong" because it implies that you'll have to exert extra effort to be persuaded that you're wrong. It doesn't feel collaborative to me. It feels like you're drawing a line in the sand and it's going to take a lot for you to cross that line. It also has a tone of condescension, and I don't think it draws your colleague in at all.

I'd rather use a phrase like "I could be totally wrong on this matter" or "I probably don't have all the information right now," which are way more self-deprecating. They're also a lot more effective if you believe them. You should.

There is a certain insecurity we feel about being wrong. It's even worse when we don't know the answer to a problem. We could feel insecure when someone who is nontechnical comes up with a great technical solution.

You have to understand that the value you bring at this point is not a technical one; it is the ability to ask the right questions in order to collaborate on finding the best solution together. The sooner you learn that nontechnical people are an asset to you, a tool in your tool chain, the more loved you'll be and the easier it will be for people to trust your judgment.

EMBRACE A LEARNING MINDSET

There is a crucial moment in any conversation I have with someone where I stop spending energy on promoting my ideas and I divert that energy to learning from the person. What makes them tick, what are they trying to accomplish, where did they first use this approach, what makes them happy in life, and how did they get to this point?

This is a great tip for you as well. As they are describing their solution, you're not folding your arms in a stone-faced judgmental posture. Rather, you are affirming and actively listening to their description. Think of it as pushing the gas pedal with them, building on their ideas and solutions in an inquisitive way and asking for clarification where needed, but playing out the solution with them.

It is important at this point to listen to the words they're using. No, we're not hacking the conversation, and we're not going to use their own words against them. We are going to understand the paradigm they're in so that we can draw a better sandbox around why they think the way they do. But it's also extremely valuable to learn the words they're using so that when you communicate with them, you're using the same words.

Personally, I would refrain from taking notes here. It's disruptive and, in some cases, could make the person you're contending with feel like you're building a case against them. I don't think it demonstrates that you think their thoughts are important in this instance, although it does at other times.

Remember that at this stage, you're choosing to learn as much about their proposed solution as possible, as if it were the only well-thought-out solution on the table.

BUILD A BRIDGE

First of all, please notice how this is not step 1!

So many times, the people we talk with, including ourselves, are blissfully oblivious of the assumptions we're making. Not only that, but also of how many factors need to go our way for our proposed solutions to work. You have a great opportunity here to highlight those assumptions without being perceived as stubborn.

Decide on all the aspects of their proposed solution that you agree with. Talk about the ideas you love, and reaffirm those to the person. This will set the stage for common questions that need to be answered. You bring the person into the current reality and propose that there are questions that can't be answered and that you'd both like to get those answered.

Build the list. Here are some examples:

- "We don't know if the customer success department will be happy with adding an extra step to their workload. We'd want to learn from them whether they think this is a solid step forward."

- "We don't know how reliable the integration will be, since this adds another step of potential vulnerability to our process. We'd want to understand if what we stand to gain is greater than the potential risk."

- "This tool introduces a whole new business process that could impact other areas that we might not be aware of at this point. We'd want to learn more about how that could complement or detract from what's working today."

See what you just did there? You formed a team! If all goes well, you and your sparring partner have just joined the same side in finding a common quest to answer the unknowns.

You won't be forming teams or doing yourself any favors if all you do at this point is poke holes in their thinking. Remember, your goal here is to work on getting them to suggest out loud what was your idea all along.

SOW YOUR IDEAS

You have successfully activated your counterpart from adversary to team member and collaborator in addressing and solving common unknowns. Depending on how you did, the person has already forgotten their love for their tools and is now a blank slate for helping you help them help you help them.

It's time to sow the seeds of your ideas.

Not all interactions are this smooth, however. There will be the following scenarios:

YOU DISAGREE

Your task here is to educate, not to patronize. Assume that you have a set of facts or frameworks that they don't know about. Vulnerability will go a long way here to explain why you think the way you do—perhaps draw on past experiences—but I would nurture the relationship with this person rather than go toe to toe on the cognitive battleground. Chances are you just don't think or reason the same way, and therefore you're arriving at different conclusions.

Your job here is to reassure, nurture, and invest in the relationship. I would suggest two ways you can use this situation to invest in the relationship while also protecting the company from pending doom:

- Bring another voice into the conversation, and ask them how the proposed solution would affect them. You'd be surprised at how often others can fight your battles for you. Sometimes proposed solutions will create more work for other people—bring those voices into the conversation.

- Offer them a sandbox in which they can try it out themselves for a trial period.

YOU PARTIALLY DISAGREE

Let's say there are some aspects you love, but you need to move the other person away from their idea and over to yours. Imagine there are dots inside of a blob. The blob is their idea, and your dots are the various points of light inside the blob that you feel you agree with. Your mission is to expand your dots, ever so gently, so that they eventually consume, destroy, or complement their blob.

YOU'VE BEEN CONVINCED

It is possible that after hearing them out, you'll get to a place where you think the idea might work overall and it's a good idea. This is the best-case scenario, and it does happen. The key here, however, is to avoid being too arrogant. Admit when you hear a good idea, and recognize it for what it is out loud. There is never anything wrong with giving someone else a win.

In this chapter you learned the Flying with Your CEO Framework for showing up as your best self when every part of you wants to excuse yourself from an ideas meeting. We also took a look at how to deal with interrogations in the C-suite without sacrificing your executive presence. Next up, we take a closer look at how to deal with failures, feedback, and conflict.

17

CONSIDER THE ROLE OF FAILURE

THERE WILL BE TIMES WHEN YOU WILL FAIL. YOU MIGHT MISS a deadline or not have the tools you thought you had to complete a job. Perhaps you've said something by mistake, or perhaps you gave away too much information before you knew all the facts. It happens. Let's consider how to prepare for the inevitability of a failure.

I think there are ways in which we deal with these disappointments. If we consider the fact that this is a long-term appointment, we realize that we are beginning to settle into a rhythm. We are getting the information we need to know the company intricately. We know the people on a personal level, and we've had our quick win. People are trusting us. We have a base to recover from mistakes, and that's important to remember.

Another important thing to keep in mind is the fact that the CEO will respond to failure differently than you. You are closer to the failure because you committed it. You might even have seen it coming.

The CEO, however, doesn't see it that way. He or she simply sees a promise not kept and might wonder if you're worth the money and hype. Maybe you negotiated a higher salary, and the CEO is beginning to regret agreeing. Maybe they were burned by a previous CTO. Whatever the reason, your CEO is going to have a reaction, and you need to be prepared for that as well.

Before making promises, understand your timeline. You've taken the time to get to know the company, and you have previous experience that should help you determine the scope and timelines of the task at hand.

As the CTO, you don't get to ask for open-ended time frames in the name of innovation or the unpredictability of software development. You should still be able to give an expert opinion on time frames. A classic example of this scenario is the dreaded, "How long will it take to build a feature?" Based on historical data and a solid dose of ignorance, the stakeholders might expect a feature to take a few weeks, when really, it would take a few months. Be prepared with this information to avoid a failure in the first place.

Failures happen and play a role in your overall performance. If you can predict them and discuss them with the affected people ahead of time, the blow might not be so bad. For example, when timelines on developing a feature slip, tell the stakeholders what's going on. Be ready with contingency planning. They will trust that you are addressing problems in a proactive manner rather than waiting and reacting when the feature is due. If you're lucky, you'll get some helpful feedback when failures happen.

These concepts may seem basic, but I know how it goes. I am a CTO; I know how this feels. Taking it on the chin when you break the bad news sucks, especially when there is always hope that the feature could be delivered on time. It's a wager, and you're on the losing end.

The temptation is to avoid the conflict now, hope for the best, and then when "disaster" strikes, find a plausible reason for why the dates slipped. I believe this is one of the most important ceilings that needs to be broken through. Share bad news up front to maintain that trust you built in the beginning.

REACTING TO FAILURE

Before we discuss how we react to failure, we first must discover how we internalize failure. Biologically, we internalize our mistakes and are apt to make more in the future. Our concentration decreases, and we run the risk of sabotaging ourselves. When we fail once, no matter how small, we run a high chance of failing again. However, we are no longer a species enslaved to our instincts. We are higher-thinking beings, and we have tools to help us best react to failure:

Don't dwell on it. The advice "learn from your failures" can become a fixation fast. Yes, learn from what you've done wrong, but also learn to let it go immediately after. Internalizing failure hurts our problem-solving skills, so instead of dwelling on it, learn to reframe it into a lesson. As with an article, there has to be a small takeaway in the longer narrative. You need to forget the overall narrative and stick with that small, one-sentence takeaway.

Don't wing a solution. You might be tempted to say "screw it" and go a different direction, trying to overcome your fear of failure. However, this doesn't work because there's no plan in place. You're winging it, wandering around with no goal in sight, trying to avoid the previous failure. You're setting yourself up to fail again. Instead, try setting specific goals to help you overcome your mistake.

Be kind to yourself. After we fail, we don't want to do that again. However, saying to yourself, "Don't do that, or you'll end up back where you were," is avoiding the issue that got you here in the first place. You're building anxiety within yourself when you do this. Instead, create positive goals and celebrate every victory, no matter how small.

Consider handling failure as a retrospective. What software developers like to do as part of the sprint process is something called a retrospective, where they take a look back at what worked for them, what didn't work, and what they can take into the next step. They ask themselves, "How are we going to approach the next sprint?"

You're leaving failure behind and building from the key takeaway. You're letting the failure fade in your memory while improving upon the lesson it taught. Meanwhile, you're setting yourself up for success by allowing only positive goals to occupy your mind and by celebrating every win.

REACTING TO FEEDBACK

As you worked through the third month, you may have had to start defending your reason for being there. Perhaps your initial wins aren't providing the results they promised. Perhaps you've had a tough time finding the data you need to create another win. Maybe your strategy isn't going to plan, or your team has poked holes in it. Whatever it is, you're going to have to reflect on your feedback to help you solve these issues.

The honeymoon phase is over, so people are sugarcoating things less. We spoke about getting feedback; now we need to discuss how you honestly react to it. We mentioned before that reacting positively was best, but what happens if your reaction wasn't always completely positive? Let's reflect on the past three months and find out how we can improve our reactions to feedback.

Let's begin by looking at the four common ways people react to feedback in general.

They treat it as a threat. This is when they become combative and enter fight-or-flight mode. Their brains sense an attack even if there is no attack, and they react emotionally.

They change the information. This is an argument back to the person giving feedback. You debate, challenge, or dismiss the information received.

They shoot the messenger. People who do this attack the person delivering the message, even when the feedback is being delivered on behalf of another person.

They look for confirmation. They look for their friends. People are looking to others to offset the feedback. This often manifests itself as someone saying to someone else, "I'm not really like that, am I?"

Where do you fall on this list? Be honest with yourself, and if you don't know, find out. The only way to learn how to respond to feedback in a way that makes you look good is to understand where you begin.

As I mentioned before, it's important to respond to feedback positively. Let's go deeper into that thought as we reflect on your first three months with this company.

Gauge your first reaction—and stop it. Stop everything you're doing—including your initial reaction to the feedback. Try to not react to it, physically, verbally, or mentally. You have one second to do this, so practice it in other areas of life before it becomes an issue at work. Are you annoyed with the slow driver in front of you? Take a second and stop your reaction. When you do this enough, it happens naturally in front of the CEO.

Remember its benefits. We reviewed the benefits of feedback before. Go back to that review. Remember that feedback is the best way to learn, and you are someone who continues to learn, right?

Listen to understand. You did it—you avoided that knee-jerk, fight-or-flight reaction. Congratulations! Now you're listening to hear what the other person is saying. Do not interrupt, and repeat back what was said to make sure all parties understand the feedback clearly.

Say thanks. This sounds hard, but it's worth it. Genuinely thank the person for the feedback. You are showing him or her respect, and you're communicating that you appreciate the time it took to evaluate your performance.

Ask questions. You want to come away from this with a clear head and a deeper understanding of why the person came to you in the first place. Make sure you have this clarity before walking away from the conversation.

Look back on all the times you've received feedback. How did you handle it? Did you follow the tips above? If you didn't, try again. Keep in mind that we are all human, we all make mistakes, and we are all a work in progress. If receiving feedback is a weakness for you, don't worry. Just keep practicing using these tips and remember that practice makes nearly perfect.

HANDLING CONFLICT

How have you handled conflict over the past three months? Are you reactive or proactive? What do you do when the CEO reacts to certain information, whether it's deadlines being missed, someone quitting unexpectedly, a strategy changing, or you forgetting to send regular updates? Often, you are put into a position where you have to react. How do you handle these situations?

Similar to handling feedback, there is a simple outline for handling conflict:

Talk to the other person. Find a convenient time and place for both of you to meet where you won't be interrupted. Make sure it doesn't butt up against any other meetings so there isn't the pressure of a time constraint.

Focus on the event, not the personality. Use phrases such as "when this happens" instead of "when you do." You don't want to put the person on the spot. You also want to use specific instances instead of general statements to help the other person see exactly what's caused the conflict.

Listen carefully. Avoid the temptation to get ready to react. Hear every word that's said thoroughly. A great way to do this is to pause at the end of the other person's sentences. This gives you a chance to know that he or she is completely done speaking before you respond. Rephrase what the other person has said and ask questions where necessary.

Identify points of disagreement and agreement. Summarize these. Ask if the other person agrees that these are the areas of contention. Modify these points until you come to an agreement about what caused the conflict.

Prioritize. Decide together what areas need the most work and focus on correcting them in the future.

Follow through. Make sure you're following through with the plan. You've both worked hard to meet in the middle. Hold on to that collaborative attitude.

Build on that success. Point out areas of progress and compliment the other person's insights. Congratulate each other on steps toward resolution until you find a way to collaborate positively.

In this chapter we faced undesirable topics like unexpected failure, unwanted feedback, and nasty conflicts. We turned each one of these into powerful tools that make us better. How we show up when things aren't going our way is everything. Everyone watches to see how you will react, and they invariably draw their conclusions. Hopefully they will be inspired by your disposition. And hopefully you'll be inspired by the final chapter! Never, and I mean never, ever, forever, never stop learning.

•

18

MAKE A GREAT CTO

So far, you've been building relationships within the company. Now it's time to pull out good stuff and really lean on what makes you shine as a CTO. There are four *T*s and four *S*s that you can use to position yourself at the top of your game. Let's start with the four *T*s:

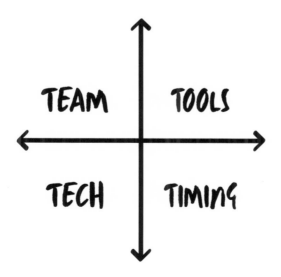

Team. It is your job to pull together a great team. You want people to become aligned with your ideas as well as with the company goals. Find people who do this well and make them a part of your team.

Tools. Give the team what they need. What might they use for empowerment and success? You are the tech person; you know what technology will work best for your strategy.

Tech. This is a no-brainer, but it remains an essential part of the quadrant. As you know, many companies simply aren't using it right. Let's fix that.

Timing. Understand when to embrace what. Is a fire actually a fire, or is it an issue that can wait until next week? When do you work on what?

Now let's investigate the four Ss. This comes after you've worked on the four Ts. Revenue is going up, tech is in place, and you're ready to scale. This chart may not be useful in the first month, but it's an important, direct extension of the four Ts and needs to be tied to them.

Shield. What are the specific technological solutions that set you apart from the competition? What have you done to make yourself stand out? How do you secure and protect this technology?

Stretch. This is also called "creating space." You want to start stretching your team into something that works better for the company. Take off hats and instead look at expertise. Is there something someone might do to benefit the company that they're currently not doing simply because it's not in their job description? Make changes where necessary.

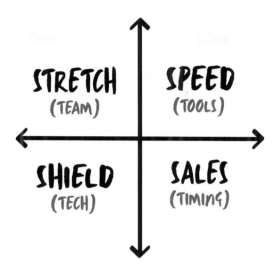

Speed. What can you do as CTO to keep the team moving forward? What tools are you using to keep the strategy moving forward? Where might you get stuck, and how do you make sure that doesn't happen?

Sales. How are you thinking about everything together to generate more sales? The Scaling CTO mindset begins as revenue builds, so help yourself get to that mindset through figuring out how to build more sales.

Finally, we have the formula that makes the CTO extraordinary:

You want to be extraordinary in implementation, you want to be the voice of innovation, and you want to be inspirational. Develop these traits by focusing on the three pillars: technology, network, and leadership.

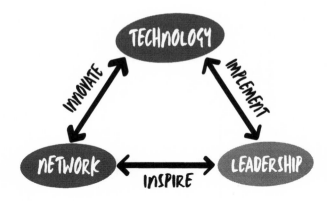

Technology. No one will ever be at fault for thinking of you as a technical person. Focus on all the aspects that keep your feet on the ground: the tools, scaling, alignment, teams, and where the technology is going.

Leadership. What are your leadership skills? How are you showing up as an emotionally intelligent person? How are you running the team? How is the team responding?

Network. You obviously have a well-developed network, and you have a voice within that network.

How do the pillars all play together to develop these three qualities? If you look at technology and leadership, combining them, you will find yourself strong in implementation. You can speak up and propose plans when necessary.

If you combine technology and network, you have a strength in innovation. You have the ability to bounce ideas off your strong network and to effectively receive feedback about those ideas.

You have the ability to be challenged and to come away from that challenge having learned something.

When you combine network with leadership, you're developing an ability to inspire. You know a lot of people through your network, and you have the ability to lead them. This is how you inspire others.

When you focus on the pillars of technology, network, and leadership, the things in between fall into place naturally. Before you know it, you've moved beyond a Startup CTO to a Scaling CTO in no time.

NEVER STOP LEARNING

Business leaders need to prioritize self-development and constantly renew their skills. When you prioritize self-improvement and a continuous learning attitude, you become someone who can weather any storm. No matter if an economy tanks, a supplier suddenly goes under, the company comes under fire publicly, or a vast pandemic strikes the planet, you will have the knowledge to survive based on your ability to keep learning.

Keep learning as much as you can through every interaction, and keep updating your CTO journal. You're not only teaching yourself about how the business works—you're also becoming a knowledgeable person to talk to when you speak to people in different functional areas.

You also gain some authority because people start to see you as someone who has a learning disposition. We all like people who want to learn. If you're communicating to others that you want to learn, you come across as more personable and more willing to fit in. Send the message that it's fine if the new company doesn't do things a certain way. You've come in with plausible deniability, and that can be used as a tool to gain more information.

Plausible deniability, used in this sense, is a deniability of knowledge of an entity. It has negative connotations in legalese, but used here, it simply means that you don't know because you've never been associated with this organization before. How could you have known that the CFO had previously dated the COO? During the first 100 days, you will use this as a tool to help you gather knowledge and get to know your team.

Plausible deniability helps you dig deeper during these conversations and often convinces people to give you more information. You are in a position to say, "Oh, I didn't know the head of engineering wasn't holding weekly meetings with the CEO," opening up a pathway for the other person to tell you why that isn't happening. People love to educate, and since you're open to learning, they will be far more willing to reveal things to you.

That deniability, combined with an obvious desire to learn, will help you find issues such as lack of communication between engineering and the CEO. This is exactly why you are talking to everyone in the first three months.

I believe that you're bringing a net positive vibe into the C-suite. That both is unusual coming from a tech person and brings a more collaborative vibe. You're saying, "Listen, I know that you're in marketing, or sales, or finance, and you feel separated from product engineering right now, but what if we could build in some tools that will help you? What if we could get the data you need that is only available in our system? What if I helped you collaborate with people?"

You've started to give them the vibe that your existence in their company will help them be successful. There is a way to prepare yourself by showing people that you want them to succeed so, in turn, you will succeed. There are few things in life as frustrating for executives as getting the data out of the system. That's where you step in. You've used your personal values (helping people and solving problems) to align with the company and its future.

What type of agreements are you making with yourself in order to make sure that you stay above the situation and don't sink down into being manipulated or being managed by people in a way that makes you unhappy? How are you effectively serving yourself and the company to help you both rise to the top? Keep noting the answers to these questions in your CTO journal to ensure your time with the company is good for both you and them.

Recognize your shortcomings as well, and work to fix them. If you're still striving to move from a Startup CTO to a Scaling CTO, realize that you might have more to learn. If your weakness is finance, for example, look to the local community college for a course in basic finance. This should begin before month one, but it's here because learning is an ongoing process.

After you learn the basics, realize the golden opportunity you have to continue your education through the experts—your coworkers. The CFO has a lot to teach, and you have a lot to learn. Through every day, every week, and every month, you should be continuing to learn. You should be building on what you already know and learning as much as possible as you go.

You learn not only through college courses, but through life. Meetings and one-on-one conversations have a lot to teach. Existing company handbooks have something to say. Even the way someone explains the simplest of procedures has something to teach you. When you consider every moment a coaching moment, not only for the other person, but also for yourself, you find yourself immersed in an ongoing education.

I find that focusing on every moment as a learning moment is a delightful way to divorce your negative feelings about colleagues from objectively looking at a specific problem at hand. If we cloud our vision with the incompetence of a colleague or their inability to clearly communicate, we grow frustrated and we shut the door on opportunities to optimize or improve processes.

It's quite remarkable what happens when you adopt this mindset. You start viewing colleagues as humans you might enjoy being around versus robots that have a malfunction that you need to destroy immediately.

That's it! You're all done! All that remains is for you to power through the conclusion. We'll take stock of the last 100 days and gaze deeply into the eyes of your future.

CONCLUSION

NOT SO LONG AGO, I ACCEPTED A CTO POSITION AT A COMPANY in desperate need of technical leadership. I got clear on my values and the personal goals I wanted to achieve at this company. I followed the outline described in this book to get up and running, and within 30 days I identified my quick win. And boy, it was a big one. In short, I saved the company from committing hundreds of thousands of dollars to build out a piece of their infrastructure that could be provided a lot cheaper and more reliably by a service provider. I just had to renegotiate the contract. In a bold move, I negotiated a very sweet deal, and everyone was thrilled.

Continuing on to days 30–40 of the 100-day model in this book, I worked on gaining a deeper understanding of their business fundamentals. I realized that there was a very big problem. In short, they were projecting income based on the assumption that customer adoption would grow exponentially after certain features were developed. Furthermore, they were paying me not from revenues but from personal loans that they had taken out and not disclosed to me. As the pressure mounted on the founders, they pushed harder for delivery dates. I broke with my personal values and started committing to delivery dates that were nearly impossible to achieve.

Ignoring the tasks outlined in this book, I pushed hard through days 40–70. I was a cheerleader to the developers, hired a VPE, and pushed through introducing my strategy for how to save the company. But the writing was on the wall. When I hit day 70, the C-suite started questioning me, and it was clear that I had lost their trust. It became harder and harder for us to navigate feedback, and my team started missing one deadline after another. In retrospect, I should have quit after the first month. But I ignored the signals and tried to save the situation. I failed.

By day 100, I was out. I had resigned after we failed to release a crucial upgrade, which caused the company to slip further into debt. Honestly, to this day, I feel really horrible about what happened. I don't know if they survived that setback.

Time and time again, I have seen how the first 100 days sets the tone for my tenure at a company. I have also been able to turn things around for myself and reinvent the CTO role at a company by following the same 100 days outlined in this book. And ultimately, following the 100 days outlined in this book has allowed me to turn down seemingly great opportunities by seeking information I normally would have ignored.

The book is broken into three parts, with the first part addressing this very issue I just shared with you: what to do before you accept the role of CTO at any company.

In Chapter 1 we discussed the importance of knowing what you want from a CTO role and the value that you bring to the company in that role.

In Chapter 2 we talked about the best ways to find CTO opportunities and the idea that being helpful is the key to growing your network. We also saw that growing your visibility inside your network creates new opportunities for you.

Chapter 3 dug into the nitty-gritty of the interview process. We saw that it can be cumbersome, but I encouraged you to be patient and to trust the process.

In Chapter 4 we discussed how you should ease into your role as CTO by resisting the urge to hit the ground sprinting.

Part 2 outlined what you should do in 100 days to establish CTO Excellence. We took it 10 days at a time, starting with Chapter 5. In Chapter 5 we took a moment to understand that you're not just accepting a role as CTO, but that you are entering an already existing system when you join a company.

Chapter 6 kicked off the 100 days with the introduction of the CTO journal, a safe and confidential medium in which you write down your answers to questions I posed throughout the book.

Chapter 7 encouraged you to have essential conversations throughout the company in order to gain an understanding of how communication flows. This gives you visibility into the system you joined and shows you what winning looks like in the company.

Chapter 8 signaled the end of your first month, where you identified the quick win. We talked about the quick win being the value you bring to the company that has great impact, but not at unreasonable cost.

In Chapter 9 you leaned on the newfound trust from your colleagues to dig deeper into the business goals with a clear handle on how the business succeeds. You are looking for sustainable growth backed by metrics that help everyone understand whether you are on track or not.

Chapter 10 acknowledged that you're having impact by this point and that there are new communication challenges you might face in the company. We talked about the "eager beavers" and how to have meaningful conversations.

Chapter 11 marked the halfway point of the 100-day model, and this was where you introduced your vision for the technology and the strategy you want to adopt in order to get there.

Chapter 12 encouraged you not to attach any negative meaning when you are asked to do menial tasks. People don't always understand what we do as CTOs, but they will take note of our willingness to help them fix the office printer!

Much like *Friday the 13th*, Chapter 13 was the movie where everything goes wrong. Business is messy, and things don't always go to plan. In this chapter we took an educated guess that by the beginning of the third month, you'll start having conversations you'd rather not have.

Chapter 14 dove into how to organize your time more efficiently, especially since the time blocks you're used to might not align with those of the company.

And rounding out the 100 days, Chapter 15 had you take a step back to engage the major stakeholders in the company so that you can understand the real purpose and motivation for the success of the company.

Part 3 of the book offered you tools for day-to-day management inside the company. We didn't dig into the actual role of the CTO, but I did give you some outlines to think about where your focus should be.

Chapter 16 discussed the challenges you might face when it comes to meetings or cross-functional initiatives that contradict your meticulous planning for technology inside the company.

Chapter 17 took a long, hard look at dealing with failure, feedback, and conflict.

We ended the book on Chapter 18, with the encouragement to never stop learning.

How have the last three months gone, honestly? Have you set yourself up for success for the rest of the year? Are you ready for the years to come? Are you happy with the progress you've made so far?

The answers to these questions are personal, and I hope they're all positive. If they're not, go back and look at how you can make changes to make them better. Perhaps at this point, you've figured out that this company isn't for you. That's okay. It happens. There are some companies, just like there are some relationships, where it just doesn't work out. If that's the case, don't be afraid to step aside and let someone else take a stab at it.

If you're happy here, though, but you don't feel like you are where you need to be, ask yourself why. Go back and review your CTO journal. What's in there that you might have missed? Where have you missed the mark?

My hope for you is that you'll be an excellent CTO, that everyone who works with you will be inspired to leave the world better than they found it. And if you find yourself lonely on the journey, please don't hesitate to reach out to me. There are many of us like you.

APPENDIX

THE PELICAN FRAMEWORK

DEVELOPED AS A WAY TO WRITE BLOG POSTS, THIS METHOD IS also highly effective in preparing presentations. It helps you answer certain questions that help you think through things in a way that's quite presentable.

I believe this is an excellent way to communicate internally because the framework raises your awareness. It provides an outside perspective that helps you see what others are seeing in your presentations. You will learn how to better position your strategy and ideas to your company and your team.

It also helps me learn if I have entered lazy thinking mode without realizing it. It helps me see if I have thought through all the different angles. If I start a presentation or blog and can't answer half the questions it presents, I know I'm in lazy thinking mode and need to find more answers.

OVERVIEW

As CTOs, we all know that we need to blog. There is something magical about putting fingers to keyboard and sharing knowledge. It can also be stressful because this requires us to organize our thoughts and go the extra mile to explain concepts we may have taken for granted. It requires us to put ourselves in the shoes of our intended audience. That is, if we even know who our audience is.

BEFORE YOU BEGIN

I find that almost always, I get stuck if the following isn't clear:

- Why am I writing this article?

- Who can I imagine reading this article?

- What do I want people to do once they've read this article?

WRITING STYLE

There are a few things to remember that will help enhance your overall writing, as well as your presentations:

- "Show, don't tell." This is very helpful to build trust with your audience. A sentence showing the audience something you've learned is very different from a sentence telling people what to do.

- Use short sentences and make sure each one offers new information.

- Take an extra minute to describe the detail or to be explicit. For instance, it's different to say, "One time I was writing code that..." than to say, "In 1995, I was asked to build a device driver for a super-secret project I was working on."

Every article we put out into the world is in competition for people's attention. While we don't want to think that, heaven forbid, we need to compromise on the artistic talent to keep people reading, it is our responsibility to know this and to write accordingly.

Once we finally sit down to write, we either do a brain dump in no particular order or we spend an extraordinary time on structure, which sucks the life out of the moment. The Pelican Framework was created as a way for the busy CTO to quickly put pen to paper in a way that helps the writer organize their thoughts.

If done correctly, this also helps the reader follow along, which, in today's world, means that they got close to the conclusion of your article.

STEP 1: PROBLEM

The problem statement is the hook. There is no doubt that if you do not clearly articulate what problem you solved, people simply won't read your article. This is also an essential way to make sure that the right people are reading your article.

Some examples include:

- "Are you experiencing a slowdown in developer productivity?"

- "For years I struggled to convince my CEO to spend time and resources on technical debt."

Keep in mind that we're not trying to write the headline here; it's just a well-formed problem statement. It clearly encourages the reader, who is experiencing the same problem, to keep on reading.

STEP 2: EXPERTISE

Now that you've hooked someone with the same problem domain, you need to show them why they need to read your article. They need to feel like you've done your research, spoken with the experts, or earned the expertise to write on this topic.

Some examples include:

- "I have been leading teams in software delivery for over two decades and have worked with teams of two all the way to two hundred."

- "I spent significant time with the author of *Leaders Eat Last* and was lucky enough to ask him about these issues."

Does this mean that you always have to be the expert? No, it doesn't. It means that you need to do your homework in a way that concisely states that you know what you're talking about. This is a good place to also cite any references or books that you used in thinking about this problem.

STEP 3: LEARNING

This section describes the solution to the problem that you stated earlier. This is most often the section that we begin with when we think of writing a blog. "Wow, this is good stuff; I should tell people about this." These are good thoughts, and this is where you get to share that knowledge.

At this point, you know that the reader shares the same problem you had and trusts that you have something good to share with them. Again, focus on "showing" and not "telling."

An example could be:

"I have found that, rather than going toe to toe in the meeting, if I instead see the meeting out and connect via email after the meeting to set up a time to chat, the outcome is much more positive."

This is the first payout for your reader. They get to see the solution that you're proposing to their problem in the form of a learning moment for yourself. The question your reader should be asking here is, "This is great! But how do I apply this to my situation?"

STEP 4: ITERATE

If your learning was the sizzle, then this is the steak. This is where you show your reader the easy-to-follow, easy-to-understand steps to iterate from where they are today to where they can get to through your learning. Call it a framework, a how-to, or a step-by-step guide.

An example framework could be:

- Grab the banana.

- Peel it.

- Eat half.

- Freeze the other half.

- See great results in the morning!

Keep the following in mind when you build your framework:

- Use simple geometric shapes.

- Name it.

Here's an example of what it could look like:

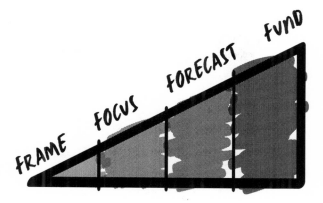

STEP 5: CONTRARIAN

At this stage, it is possible that someone might object to your framework or to your overall proposed solution. Why not spend a bit of time addressing this audience? They may actually be your target audience, but they need a gentle nudge to completely accept this method.

By spending time on possible objections, you are demonstrating that you are an authority on this subject matter, that you are able to empathize with those who don't agree with you, and that you care about those who might find it hard to apply your ideas to their situations.

STEP 6: AGAIN

It's always a good idea to repeat yourself. Be concise, and find a way to leave your reader with a few core ideas.

Simply reiterate your points by stating them differently. This is also the "takeaway"—what is the main thing you want your reader to remember from all the words he or she just consumed?

STEP 7: NEXT STEPS

Never let a good article go to waste! If someone has reached this point, you should ask something of them. It demonstrates your willingness to go deeper and your openness to take the discussion further.

ACKNOWLEDGMENTS

I WANT TO THANK KATHRYN, MY BEAUTIFUL WIFE, FOR STANDING by me during all our travels, all our challenges, and all the fun we could possibly have in one lifetime. Mostly, I am the luckiest person alive for starting each day with her. I would never have embarked on my coaching journey had it not been for observing her way as a therapist.

To Michael Saul, my co-founder at 7CTOs. I will never forget the day I pitched him and his wife, Michelle, on the idea of 7CTOs. His enthusiasm, gentleness, and raw passion were so vital to getting us started in the early years.

To Kelly Abbott, who sat me down at the Irish pub and told me I had to do 7CTOs, long before it even had a name. I'll never forget how he implored me to value myself and my experience as a CTO and to share it with the world.

André and Estelle de Bruin for blazing a trail into this world that I've been emulating since I was a young boy. Thank you for opening the door for us to make a new home in the United States.

To James Martin and Drew, for giving me my first CTO job.

To Dan Martell, who coached me into becoming an entrepreneur.

Casey Kleindienst is the closest I've had to a guru in this lifetime. He taught me the fundamentals of leadership with such wisdom that I still hear his voice in my head.

To Beth Rehberg, CEO at 7CTOs, the consummate professional. Our whole community is lucky to have her, and I can't wait to see where she'll take us next!

To my partner in coaching and all things ontological, Brittany Cotton. I am blown away by the friendship we developed in such a short time. 7CTOs is so lucky to have her as head of coaching.

To my unexpected surprise, Ilana Ingber. The de Bruin household is addicted to her love.

To my Dad, Leon de Bruin. You gave me the passion to always look for something bigger and better in this world.

To my Mom, Esme de Bruin. You gave me the confidence that comes from a mother's unbridled love.

And to all of the CTO community. If you're a CTO, I'm coming for you.

ABOUT THE AUTHOR

ETIENNE DE BRUIN has served in chief technology officer roles for over twenty years. He is the founder of 7CTOs, a peer group community for CTOs with more than three hundred members worldwide. He is the co-creator of Ekklesia360 Content Management System, which was sold to Ministry Brands in 2015. He coaches C-suites of multimillion-dollar tech companies. Etienne was born and raised in South Africa, where he got his computer science degree at Stellenbosch University. After he and Kathryn married, they moved to Germany, where Etienne built FreeBSD device drivers for proprietary encryption cards. In 2000, they moved to the USA, where they currently live with their three children.